# Return to Tybee

# A Woman's Story

## By

## Annette Bergman

ISBN: 1-4107-5715-3 (e-book)
ISBN: 1-4107-5714-5 (Paperback)

This book is printed on acid free paper.

1stBooks - rev. 06/23/03

# Chapter 1

It was Sunday morning July 4, 1982, and Kokomo, like the rest of the nation, would be celebrating with fireworks, patriotic parades and picnics. This morning entered with remnants of the previous day's heat. It was going to be another scorcher, and if I wanted to pick blackberries I knew I had to go early.

"Time to get up, Adam, we're pickin' berries this morning, remember?" He awoke with his usually sweet smile.

"Morning, Mom." Adam slowly rolled out of bed and dressed for the blackberry picking he had promised to help me with. We were planning to have a cookout later in the afternoon. I wanted to bake a fresh blackberry cobbler, partly because I liked blackberry cobbler, partly because it reminded me of my childhood, and partly because the thought of going to the woods was appealing to me after spending the past week on the road and in the hospital with my mother.

I had fond memories of picking berries with my mother and grandmother when I was a child living on a small island off the coast of Georgia. I recalled one particular berry pickin' time with my grandmother when she spotted a rattlesnake. Instead of being frightened, my grandmother said, "Ya might as well go away, Mr. Snake. These berries are mine. Paige stand real still and he'll go away." I had been impressed with the lack of fear my grandmother showed toward that rattlesnake. I was ready to drop my bucket and haul off for home, but I had been frozen with

1

Annette Bergman

fear. If I moved I would be disobeying my grandmother and that might be worse than being bitten by a diamondback rattlesnake. I recall the snake incident every time I pick berries. It seemed like, come the fourth of July, I always had to have a blackberry cobbler.

Now it looked like Mama would never pick blackberries again. The stroke had left her paralyzed on one side and the doctors weren't sure what her mental capacity was going to be. Such a simple task, picking blackberries, but it took physical and mental well being and I'm not sure that my mother would ever be in good physical or mental health again. Seeing my mother with her head shaved and paralyzed on one side had torn at the center of my soul. I had always thought that my mother would always be just a phone call away. I was losing the most stable part of my life. My mother had been there for me whenever I needed her and now I needed to be there for her. It had been hard to leave her. "Mama, I'll be back to take care of you when they let you out of the hospital," I had told her and would do just that. It was the least I could do for her.

"I can't think about that now, company's coming and I need to focus on getting things ready." It seemed that the best way for me to handle my problems was to do something I could see to completion. It gives me a sense of satisfaction. If I wasn't cooking today I would be sewing or working in my garden. *Put it off by keeping busy is my approach to life.* Today I would concentrate on company. There were plenty of berries and I picked until Adam called.

"My bucket's full. Can I stop now?" Adam's pleading voice called out.

"Mines almost full, too. I guess we had better quit. By the time we get home and get the cobbler in the oven, it will be close to 10:00 o'clock. Company'll be there at one." We walked the path back to where we had parked the car and loaded our blackberries into the trunk.

"Look how purple my hands are." Adam looked at me as though his hands would be purple for the rest of his life.

"Mine, too. That goes with pickin' berries, Adam. You'll probably find some briars in there, too. As soon as we get home I'll fix you some bleachwater. It'll take the purple off and help keep you from getting poison ivy, too."

"Do you like pickin berries?"

"It wasn't bad. I wouldn't wanta do it everyday."

"I always liked pickin' berries when I was a kid. Of course, in Georgia the berries are ripe earlier. Did I ever tell you about my grandma picking berries and running upon a snake?"

"Ya, mom, I think you told me, a couple'ah times."

"I thought maybe I had. Can't help myself I think of my grandma every time I pick berries."

We arrived home and I quickly made some bleachwater for us to wipe ourselves off. It had been fun picking berries. Adam was always very willing to help me.

"Here, Adam, use this and wipe your legs and arms." I handed him the washcloth.

"How do you know this stuff works?"

"My mother taught me to do this, and it does work. Not only does it keep you from getting poison ivy, it also bleaches the purple out of your hands." Adam smiled as we finished wiping with the bleachwater, thinking how he never heard something just once. I always told him twice.

3

"Adam, see if your dad has finished mowing, and when he finishes, help him set up the tables, okay?"

As soon as I had the cobbler in the oven I quickly made the rest of the meal while Clay prepared the grill for the cookout. If Clay hadn't had everything ready for me, there would have been no way I could have followed through with the plans for the cookout and entertaining our friends.

The company arrived and the celebration of the fourth of July was off to a good start. The aroma of the steaks sizzling on the grill was tantalizing.

I was still tired from my trip back from Tybee Island just two days before, so I was looking forward to the relaxing time of the holiday.

After everyone had eaten, Adam came into the kitchen.

"Mom, can I go pick up Billy and go swimming?"

"Sure you can, Adam. Just remember you have to be home by 11:00 p.m., okay?"

I knew how he and Billy were when they got together. Time always got away from them.

"No problem. I'll see you later. Love ya Mom." With that he was out the door. I watched as he backed his two-door Buick out of the driveway.

The curfew that the counselor had suggested had been working well for all three of us. Having a plan for the remainder of Adam's teenage years had started to relieve some of the tension that had existed between Clay and me. We had gotten along beautifully until I had gone to work selling real estate. The big problem started when Clay had bought a car for Adam without my approval. I didn't understand what my husband was thinking. "All boys need a car when they get their license," he had said, and I had vowed I wouldn't have any part of the responsibility of the car.

The rest of the holiday passed pleasantly enough. The sun went down in a fiery red ball that promised another scorcher the following day. Clay and I spent the evening watching television and relaxing. I think he had missed me while I had been in Georgia.

Clay went to bed, but I sat reading, trying to stay awake while waiting for Adam to come home. About 10:45 the phone rang.

"Hello."

"Mom, I want to come home, but Jenny is here with me and she won't leave with me."

"Adam, you know the rules. If you are not here by 11:00 you'll lose your car."

"I know, Mom, but I can't just leave Jenny here. How'll she get home?"

"Where are you, Adam?  I'll come and get Jenny," I said.

"Never mind, I'll be home in a few minutes." His voice sounded somewhat defeated. The words *I'll be home in a few minutes* kept repeating themselves to me. For some reason I had a bad feeling. There was something about the sound of his voice. I couldn't keep my mind on the magazine. Soon it was 11:30 and Adam still wasn't home. Midnight came and went. I knew for certain now that the phone would ring again. I saw myself picking it up and listening to a voice telling me Adam was dead. I had a feeling of dread as I've never had before.  I walked into the bedroom and laid down quietly beside Clay, keeping an eye on the clock.  When the telephone rang, it was 2:15 a.m. My heart started pounding.

"Hello."

"Is this the Mitchell residence?" A businesslike, unemotional voice identified itself as an officer calling from the state police station in Peru, Indiana about twenty miles from Kokomo. My heart sank and my whole body began to tremble uncontrollably when he asked me if I had a son named Adam Mitchell.

"Yes, I do," I said. My heart started to pound and my breath had an icy feel to it, like it was being blown across a glacier before coming out of my body.

"Mrs. Mitchell, we need for you and Mr. Mitchell to come to the State Police station near Peru, right away."

"What's happened?" I wanted to cry, yet I didn't want to hear the bad news, feeling that the worse fear was about to be told to me. I was afraid my son was dead.

"We need you and your husband here at the station right away," he replied.

"Could I come by myself? It's late and my husband has to go to work in the morning," I said. I hated to ask Clay to get up in the middle of the night to be involved with Adam. He was always too hard on Adam.

"I'm sorry, ma'am, but this is of a very serious nature. I need both of you here." His voice became more stern than before.

"All right, we'll be there in about thirty minutes. What is this about?"

"Mrs. Mitchell we have your son here at the State Police Post." *Then he's alive, thank God, he's alive*, I thought with joyous relief.

"Would you please come here as soon as possible." He seemed a little irritated that I had asked him questions about my son.

"We'll be there as soon as we can." I hung up the phone. Clay was awake by now. "What was all of that about?"

"Clay, it was the state police." I told him what had been said as I was grabbing a pair of white cotton slacks and a coral colored dotted Swiss blouse and slipped on my shoes. Clay grabbed a shirt and slipped on his jeans and we were out the door in what seemed like seconds and on our way to the state police post near Peru.

Clay hadn't said one word. I had hardly gotten into the car when I started speculating on what might have happened. "I wonder what's going on. I don't know why the police have to be like that. Why can't they tell you what's going on, instead of making you drive this far wondering the entire time?"

"Don't worry about it, Hon. We'll find out when we get there." The drive through Kokomo took agonizingly long. I silently prayed, "Dear God, please look after Adam." It all seemed like a dream.

"Clay, I know the counselor said we had to lay down the rules and make Adam abide by them, but Adam has been so upset lately that I don't think laying down rules is what he needs. He seems deeply troubled. When I told him he had to be home by 11:00 p.m. or he would lose his car, he just didn't seem to care one way or the other."

My stomach was knotting and my mind was racing. We were just south of Grissom Air Force Base when in the distance I saw flashing red lights.

"Clay, there must be an accident up ahead. There are a lot of flashing red lights. God, I hope Adam wasn't in an accident. Slow down, Clay. Oh, no, that's Adam's car!" I stared in disbelief.

"Stop the car, Clay!" My body started to shake uncontrollably.

"Take it easy, Hon, don't panic. We'll go over and see what's happened," he said in a comforting way.

As we walked closer to the accident site and saw the pile of rippled and twisted metal still identifiable as Adam's car, I wondered how anybody could have escaped the wreckage unhurt or even alive. The front end was smashed in and the windshield was shattered. When I looked inside the car I saw that the steering wheel was bent at an odd angle. I wondered if Adam was alive. Surely the police wouldn't take a body to the police station. I looked over at the other car and noticed people all around it. I walked toward it.

"Get back, lady, you can't go any closer," came a stern voice from a policeman.

"What happened to the person who was driving this car?" I asked.

"He's at the police post," the policeman responded with disgust in his voice. It seemed as though he knew more than he was telling.

"What about the people in the other car? Are they hurt?" I asked as I leaned to one side of the policeman to get a better look.

"Ma'am, he's dead," he said in a soft voice. He looked close to tears. Somebody moved away from the side of the car and I noticed the barely recognizable Indiana State Police emblem on the car. The rear end and top of the car were a mangled mess. I could see a body still in the car. They were trying to cut into the car to remove the body. I wanted to vomit and felt my knees giving way under me. Clay had been watching me and grabbed me by the arm and held me in an upright position before my knees gave way under me. I had been totally unaware of Clay's presence.

"Let's go to the police post, and see about Adam," Clay said with a soft loving voice. Clay continued to hold onto me while we walked back to the car with the silent fear that our son might somehow be responsible for the death of a state trooper. As we traveled the rest of the way to the police post we were both silent, each wondering what this would lead to and what we might be told when we got there.

We hurried into the police station and identified themselves as Adam's parents. An officer showed us into a small room and asked us to wait while he located the detective. Soon a man in a suit walked in and introduced himself as Detective Roberts.

"Mr. and Mrs. Mitchell, I regret to inform you that your son has been involved in an accident that has left a state trooper dead. I would suggest you contact an attorney."

"Could we see our son?" I asked.

"Yes, I'll have him brought in. After you have spoken with him you'll be welcome to use the telephone at the desk to call an attorney."

An officer returned shortly with Adam. The odor of alcohol entered the room with him. "What are you doing here? Where are we?" Adam asked.

"Adam, are you all right? Look at me. You look awful." I checked for physical evidence that Adam was all right. It only took one look into his young blue eyes to know that he looked like a stranger to his own mother. He was covered with dirt and his usually shining red hair was matted, dirty and tossed about. He appeared confused and I felt like I didn't know the person standing in front of me.

"Why are we here?" Adam asked.

"You were in an accident. Don't you remember?" It was obvious that he was dazed and frightened and wasn't in his right mind. He didn't seem to hear me.

"Why are we here? He asked again.  What happened? Where am I? I want to go home." He kept repeating this with a blank unemotional stare. I looked to Clay for comfort.  He was sitting there in almost as bad a daze as Adam.  It was obvious that Adam could have been in another world. He had no idea what had happened, and his face, red, swollen and covered with dirt lacked any expression.

"Clay, what attorney should we call?"

"I don't know any attorneys in town except the one we used when we sold the house. Why don't you call him? Wasn't his name Angel?"

"Yes, it was.  I'll give him a call and see what we're supposed to do. I'll be right back." I started to walk into the work area when I heard a trooper on the telephone say, "He made a mistake and pulled out in front of a speeding vehicle and was killed instantly."

"Excuse me, sir, would you have a Kokomo telephone book? I was told to use the telephone at the desk to make a call."

The sergeant handed me the book and I quickly found Jerry Angel's telephone number. To my surprise the telephone was answered on the second ring. "Hello, Mr. Angel, this is Paige Mitchell. I'm sorry to wake you, but I have an emergency."

"You won't believe it, but I wasn't asleep. My wife and I were up watching the eclipse. What can I do for you?"

I quickly filled him in on the situation.

"Well, what your son needs is a criminal attorney. I would suggest that you call Jim Fleming. He is a good man and he will advise you of the best thing to do."

"Thank you so much for your help and again I'm sorry for calling you at this time of the morning." I looked up Jim Fleming's number in the telephone book and gave him a call.

"Hello," came a sleepy voice.

"Hello, Mr. Fleming, my name is Paige Mitchell. I'm calling about my son. He's been in an accident that killed a state trooper. The police told me to call an attorney, I called Jerry Angel and he said I should call you."

"Mrs. Mitchell, there is nothing that can be done until we have a police report. We have to know what they're charging him with first. I'll get the report first thing in the morning. You be in my office with a $1,000 retainer fee by 10:00 a.m. There isn't anything that can be done tonight. You try and get some sleep and I'll see you in the morning."

It was obvious the conversation was over, and I wondered how Adam would handle being in jail. He was an immature seventeen-year-old, but he had a heart of gold. He loved older people and older people loved him. One of his friends' mother had told me she felt like Adam would grow up to be a minister because he was such a loving and caring person. If Adam had a hard side to him I had not seen it.

I heard the $1000 amount repeating in my mind as I slowly hung up the phone. We had put every penny into the remodeling of the home that we had just purchased. The trip to Georgia had taken additional money and I had been off work while I was with my mother. The real estate market was in a recession and my sales were not what they had been before the interest rates had gone up. I worried how we would come up with the money.

I returned to the small room where Clay and Adam were waiting, and explained to Clay that there was nothing that could be done until morning.

The detective returned to the room. "We're taking your son to the hospital for a blood alcohol test, and you're welcome to follow us if you would like."

Clay and I followed the squad car to the hospital so we could be with Adam until the test was completed. His blood alcohol level was point ten or slightly above the legal limit, had he been an adult. Adam wouldn't be an adult legally until September. As the officers prepared to take Adam back to the jail, Clay and I each told him good-bye and that we would see him the next day. The tears were running down my face as I turned to walk away. I had vowed when Adam was born that I would always protect him, but this was out of my control and my heart was breaking because my son was going to jail.

It was about 5:00 a.m. when Clay and I returned home. Clay went to bed immediately. I was numb from the night's events and sat in a dark room silently crying and wondering about the family of the dead trooper. The fact that my son had killed a man was a concept too big to grasp. Gentle, loving Adam wouldn't knowingly hurt any living thing. How could such a thing have happened? I was hoping I would awake and find this was all a bad dream. But I knew it wasn't. I knew that life for us would never be the same.

# Chapter 2

Clay had left for work a few hours before I awoke. I looked at the clock. It was 9:00 a.m. and the radio was playing softly. I was surprised that I had fallen asleep at all. In the fog of first awakening, I remembered what had happened and thought about the money I needed to take to the attorney at 10:00. I quickly made our bed and went into the kitchen where my morning coffee awaited me. Clay always made coffee for me when he got up in the mornings. Still thinking about the money for the attorney, I looked around to see if Clay had left a note or a check somewhere. Not finding one I called him at work.

"May I speak to Clay Mitchell, please?"

I waited for what seemed like hours for Clay to come to the phone.

"Hello."

"Clay, what do you want me to do about the retainer money for the attorney? I forgot to have you leave a check for him."

"I'm not taking the money I saved to go deer hunting to pay for an attorney," Clay said.

"But, Clay, how am I suppose to come up with that much money?"

"I don't know and I don't care. We have tried and tried and that boy doesn't listen. I am not helping him anymore." I could hear anger in his voice that was foreign to me. Clay was normally a quiet person. This sudden anger had surprised me.

Without another word I hung up the telephone. I looked in my address book for my brother-in-law's work telephone number. I could hardly see through the tears to dial the number. I didn't know what was wrong with Clay. He had bought the car for Adam but now he wasn't willing to help him.

"Savannah Glass Company, how may we help you?" said a cheerful southern voice.

"May I speak to Gordon Smith please?" I was put on hold a moment. "Hello, this is Gordon."

"Gordon, it's Paige. I didn't know who to call. I didn't dare call Daddy at the hospital. We can't let Mama know about this."

"What's wrong?"

"Adam had a wreck. He hit and killed an Indiana State trooper. It happened around two this morning. They have him in jail and I need some money to pay a retainer fee to an attorney. Clay won't give me the money. I want to borrow it from Daddy, but I was afraid to call him at the hospital. Mama might want to know what is going on and I'm afraid it would kill her at this point. Could you go to the hospital and get Daddy out in the hall and ask him if he would wire me the money? Tell him I will pay it back as soon as I have a closing. Also tell him not to let Mama know. All she needs to be doing is concentrating on getting well. I'm afraid if she hears about Adam's wreck she might have another stroke. It could kill her.

"Was Adam hurt in the accident?"

"I'm not sure. Last night he just kept asking, 'Where am I? What happened?' They took him to the hospital for a blood alcohol test but they didn't examine him to see if he was hurt. I want to go see him again after I talk with his attorney. I have an appointment at 10:00 this morning."

"I'll send you the money. We'll worry about paying it back later. How much do you need and where do I send it?"

I gave him the details and hung up the telephone. I was touched by how concerned Gordon was for Adam, and how he didn't hesitate to send me the money. Gordon had always been very good to my family. I felt embarrassed that Clay wouldn't give me the money. I was beginning to get angry about it. I felt relieved that I had the money to pay for an attorney for Adam. I showered and dressed to make my 10:00 appointment. I was always on time for my real estate appointments and I wasn't going to be late for this appointment either.

I was the only one in the waiting room at Jim Fleming's office. I pretended to be looking at a magazine when the receptionist showed up and asked me to come into Jim's office.

"Good morning Mrs. Mitchell, I'm sorry we are meeting under these circumstances. I talked with the detective this morning and I was told that the trooper was the father of two small children. What a tragedy for all concerned. The first thing I want you to do is write to the widow, Mrs. Lather, and express your sorrow for what has happened. I'll need to talk to Adam and find out what they are charging him with in Peru. There's talk that they're charging him with running a stop light in Howard County. If that's true, we can plead guilty to running the stop light and they'll not be able to charge him with anything in Miami County," Jim said.

"Two small children," echoed in my head. "Those children will never know their father. I don't know what to say. I'm so upset that Adam is involved in something like this. He is such a gentle kid. He wouldn't harm anyone. I don't know how he'll ever be able to live with this. I'll write Mrs. Lather a letter, but I'm not sure anything I have to say will be a comfort to her right now, or ever, for that matter." My knees began a slow quiver. My stomach started burning.

"Jim, I didn't bring your retainer with me, I have to borrow it from my father who lives in Georgia. He's at the hospital all day long with my mother. She had a stroke about ten days ago and almost died. They had to do brain surgery and she's still in critical condition. I just came back from Georgia on Saturday."

"Is your mother going to be all right?"

"It's too soon to tell. The doctors think she'll be paralyzed on her left side. They're not sure how much brain damage there's going to be. I'll have your money here sometime this afternoon. My brother-in-law is having it wired here today. I'll bring it by as soon as it arrives. I would like to see Adam today if I can."

"Sure. I'll be going to Peru shortly after lunch. I'll meet you at the jail around 1:30 p.m. and we'll talk to him together. Will your husband be joining us?"

"I doubt it. He's working. In the factories if you don't work the day after a holiday, you aren't paid for the holiday. I'll meet you at the jail in Peru at 1:30. Jim, is there anything else that I can do? I feel so helpless." I tried not to cry but the tears were running down my cheeks.

"Not now. Just don't forget to write that letter immediately," Jim said as he opened the door for me and gently placed his arm around my shoulder as if to say he understood my grief.

I didn't want to go to my real estate office. I wasn't sure what I wanted to do, so I headed home, wiping the tears from my cheeks as I drove, my mind in a spin. I remembered that I was supposed to show homes to a client in the afternoon. As soon as I arrived home and poured myself a cup of coffee I picked up the phone to call the office.

"Good morning, Homes for Living."

"Hi, Penny, is Brian in?"

"Yes, he's here. Is something wrong? You sound awful."

"Penny, I don't know if I have the strength to tell this twice. Let me speak to Brian and he can tell you."

"Just a minute, I'm going to put you on hold," said Penny, wondering what was going on.

"Morning Paige. What's up?" Brian asked.

"Brian, my son was in a horrible accident last night. I'm not sure about the details, but a state trooper was killed and my son is in jail. I have clients coming in at 2:00 to look at three homes. Could you get someone to cover for me?"

"Don't worry about the clients. I'll take care of it for you. How's your son?"

"I'm not really sure. I'll be going to see him after lunch. Last night he didn't seem to understand what was going on. He had been drinking and I couldn't tell if it was the alcohol or if he was in shock. I've never seen him in that condition. I'll call you after I see him and have some idea of when I will be coming back to work. And thank you, Brian, for taking care of my clients. I appreciate it." I gave him the information about my clients and thanked him again.

17

Without waiting for a response, I quickly hung up the telephone.

I found my pen and paper and after making several attempts I wrote:

Dear Mrs. Lather,

I hope this letter isn't upsetting to you. It certainly isn't intended to be. Being the mother of the young man who was involved with the death of your husband, I felt compelled to write to you.

Just to say I'm sorry is not enough. You and your children are continuously in my thoughts and prayers. I'm sure no one fully understands the pain you're suffering. I've thought about you ever since I found out Trooper Lather was married and had two children. I feel so helpless.

I know God must have a plan for all of us in the future and it's that plan that will get me though the days ahead. I pray God will be with you and your family and give you strength and comfort when you face each morning.

If there is anything I can do for you, please call me. I really would like to meet you and your children, but I can understand any feeling you might have. I do want you to know that regardless of what happens with all the legal aspects, I know you've suffered a tremendous loss and nothing can replace a husband and father.

My heart goes out to you. I pray if we ever meet, that you will find that we are not your enemies. We have suffered, too. May God bless you and keep you in His care.

Sincerely,
Paige Mitchell

I slowly folded the letter, moistened the envelope, sealed it, and wiped the tears from my eyes. That had been one of the most difficult things I'd ever had to do. Those poor people, how sad they must be feeling, and their sadness would be with them for the rest of their lives. This accident had destroyed the hopes and dreams of many people. I took the letter to the mailbox and left for Peru to meet Jim Fleming.

As I drove, I thought about Clay's attitude and wondered how this whole situation would affect our lives. The thought that this tragedy would sound the death knell for our already faltering marriage was quickly brushed to the back of my mind. I thought of Scarlet O'Hara from *Gone with the Wind* and said aloud, "I'll think about that tomorrow."

# Chapter 3

In 1961 Jack and I were together constantly. I knew Jack was the love of my life, but I wasn't sure if Jack felt the same, even though he seemed truly happy when we were together. We both liked the song "Our Day Will Come," and I secretly believed it. Once when Jack and I had gone to Kings Island, we were both laughing and having a good time. Jack had put his arms around me and kissed me softly, saying, "I Love you Butterfly," and I had built an imaginary future on those words. I had grand fun with him. Who could have known the outcome would be so painful?

When I returned from one of my trips to visit my parents in Georgia, Jack had asked me to come into his office.

"Please close the door, Paige," Jack said in a serious voice.

At first, I thought he was just stealing a little time to be with me. One look at his face told me it was something serious.

"I have something to tell you. I know you're going to be upset, but I want you to hear it from me." His voice sounded apologetic.

"You remember the girl I told you about. The one who followed me all the time?" Jack asked.

"I remember."

"Well, she's pregnant and is claiming the baby's mine."

"Well, is it your baby?" I demanded.

"I don't know. I guess there is a chance it could be."

"What do you mean, you guess? All this time I've been thinking that you weren't seeing anybody but me, and now you tell me, *you think* you could be the father of her child?" I screamed, thinking to myself of how I should never trusted Jack or any other man for that matter.

"Now, Paige, before you get really upset let's wait until the baby is born. We'll go over there together and you tell me if you think the baby is mine. Faye goes out with a lot of guys. It could be someone else's baby."

Jack had gotten up from his desk and was coming toward me. He reached out and pulled me into a standing position, taking me into his arms.

"Paige, you know I don't want anything to happen to us. Please be patient with this and it'll all work out," Jack whispered as he leaned down to kiss my moist eyelids.

I responded as Jack had hoped I would. I raised my head. A kiss was all it took for Jack to make it better.


Months later when the baby was born the two of us had gone over to see Faye and her newborn child. It was awkward for me. Faye didn't seem like the harassing person Jack had made her out to be. She had beautiful green eyes that had a sad look to them and sandy brown hair. I thought she was quite attractive. The baby looked just like Jack, long and lanky with blond hair.

Faye handed me the baby. "Jack, I need to speak to you in the bedroom." I tried hard to hear what was being said but couldn't. I started talking to the baby and thinking how wonderful it would be to have one of my own someday. After a few minutes they returned and Jack said. "Let's go." I handed the baby to Faye and said good-bye.

Once outside Faye's apartment, I turned to Jack.

"Jack, the baby looks just like you. I think the thing for you to do is marry her and make a home for your son." I was very stern. It wasn't how I had hoped our relationship would end, but I felt the baby needed a father more than I needed Jack.

"I don't want to do that. I want you," Jack said without hesitating.

"Well, it's a little late for that. You didn't want me too bad or you wouldn't have been out with Faye."

Jack tried to reason with me. "You were in Georgia, I was drinking and I've told you how she kept chasing me. It just happened. It's not like I planned it."

I remained silent as we returned to the insurance office. Jack reached for the mail on his way into his office. A few minutes passed and Jack called for me to come into his office.

"Talk about timing. I have just been notified that I have been drafted and I have to report in less than two weeks," Jack said.

"That's just perfect, you can walk away from me and Faye," I snapped.

"Please, let's just spend as much time as we can together before I have to leave. This'll all work out, I promise," Jack reassured me. "I had better call the home office so they can find a replacement." He picked up the telephone and I walked out of the room feeling deserted and betrayed.

Jack made all the arrangements and within what seemed like no time to me, he was on his way to boot camp.

Weeks passed and Jack wrote faithfully. I really missed him. I hated to go to work; it wasn't fun without Jack around. Jack didn't mention Faye and the baby in his letters and I didn't ask any questions. It was easier not to talk about the problem that was between us. Somehow I felt if I didn't talk about the problem they would resolve themselves or just mystically disappear.

The weeks seemed to drag by and I felt like I was dragging with them. Since Jack had left, all the fun in my life had left with him. I didn't have any energy and wasn't eating the way I normally did. I was tired all the time and had lost weight. I made an appointment with the doctor.

They called my name and showed me into a small room with an examination table in it.

The nurse asked several questions, then said, "Please remove all of your clothes and slip this on, so the doctor can examine you."

I laid down on the table while waiting for the doctor. He entered the room and quickly introduced himself.

"I'm Dr. Rabhand. I understand you're not feeling well."

"I'm not. I just feel tired all the time and I feel sick to my stomach a lot."

"How long have you been feeling exceptionally tired?" asked Dr. Rabhand.

"It's been several weeks. I really can't remember."

"Before we do a lot of tests, I would like to do a physical examination." He called in a nurse and he started the examination. He looked in my ears, he checked my eyes, felt around my neck and made his way down my tired body.

"Just what I thought. You're pregnant. I would say at least two months. When was the last time you had a monthly period?"

"I don't remember. I've had a lot on my mind and I guess I just didn't think about it," I said choking back the tears.

23

"Aren't you happy about being pregnant, Paige?"

"I'm not sure. I've always wanted children. I just thought I would be married before I started having them." I felt my face redden as the doctor helped me into a sitting position on the examination table.

"Where's the father of the child?" asked Dr. Rabhand.

"He's in boot camp at Fort Campbell, Kentucky."

"Perhaps when you tell him you're going to have his baby he'll be happy and you two can get married. I'm going to start you on some vitamins and I would like to see you back in here in one month." The doctor said, then left the room.

\* \* \*

A horn sounded, and I found myself sitting still at a green light. I quickly pulled away and started looking for the Peru jail. Peru wasn't a very large town. It was famous for being Cole Porter's home and the summer quarters for the Ringling Brothers' Circus. In fact it was called "The Circus City." Clay had brought Adam and me to Peru for a parade one year when Adam was just a little boy. The parade was filled with floats, and there had been lots of animals. Clay seemed especially proud to be sharing his world with us that day. *Funny how bad times help you to remember the good years*, I thought as I pulled up across the street from the jail, parked the car and walked inside where I found Jim Fleming waiting for me.

"Hi, Jim. Have you been waiting long?"

"No, I just got here. They said it would be just a few minutes and we could see him."

Shortly a guard escorted the two of us into a room where Adam sat looking pale and frightened. I gave him a hug.

"Adam, this is Mr. Jim Fleming. He's going to be your attorney."

"Hi, Adam. How'ya doing?"

"I don't know. I feel sick," he said softly.

"Why don't you tell me what happened," Jim suggested.

"I don't remember."

"You don't remember anything about the accident?"

"No sir, I don't. Someone told me this morning that I killed a man." The tears ran down his face.

"Tell me the last thing you remember," Jim said.

"I was in my car and the radio was playing *Old Flame*. All I could think about was Jenny. I wanted to find her."

"Where were you going, Adam?"

"I was looking for my girlfriend. She wouldn't leave the party with me. I started to go home alone and I turned around to go back for her. When I got back to where the party was, she was gone. Someone said she'd left with two boys, and I was afraid of what they might do to her. I drove by her house, and she wasn't home. I thought maybe they had taken her to the Mississinewa Reservoir, and I was on my way there. That's all I remember."

"Were you drinking at the party?" Jim asked.

"Yes, sir," Adam answered dropping his head and looking toward the floor.

"Where was the party, and where did you get the alcohol?" asked Jim.

"It was at Billy's house. His uncle bought it for us."

Jim looked to me to see if I had some idea of who Billy, or Billy's uncle was. I gave a slight nod to indicate that I could fill in some blanks for him.

"Adam, do you remember the police chasing you?" Jim asked.

"I don't remember the police chasing me at all. If the police had been chasing me I would have pulled over."

"Do you remember any red lights in front of you?" Jim hammered away.

"No, sir, I didn't see any red lights. Mom, you know me. I would have stopped if I had seen any red lights."

"You try to get some rest and I'll get back with you later," Jim said.

I gave my son a kiss on the forehead. "I love you, Adam. We'll get through this, I promise," I said as I wiped away his tears. It was breaking my heart to see my son locked away in jail. Adam was such a kind and loving person, this wasn't the way things were supposed to be for him. I was always going to love him enough for two people and see to it that he had a good life. How could this be happening?

Jim and I walked outside and stood talking on the sidewalk in front of the Peru jail.

"I'll want you to come into my office as soon as I have a written report on this accident. It seems there were some witnesses. Who is Billy and what's his uncle's name?"

"Billy is Adam's best friend. He's also the son of a good friend of mine. I can't think of his uncle's name, but I'll get it for you."

"I'll try to get a bail set and get back with you as soon as I know something," Jim promised.

"Thanks for taking the case, Jim. Call me at home when you know something. I don't feel like going back to work yet. You should be able to get me at any hour. Just let the phone ring. I might be outside." I knew myself well enough to know I had to work in the garden to get my thoughts together and do some praying while I was on my knees. It was going to take a lot of prayers to get through this.

As soon as I returned home I called my friend Carol.

"Hello."

"Hi, Carol. I don't know if you've heard yet, but Adam had an accident last night. He hit and killed a state trooper."

"Oh, my God, is Adam hurt?" Carol asked.

"I don't think so, not physically anyway. Carol, I need to talk to you."

"I'll be right there." I replaced the receiver in its cradle and took a deep breath.

"Billy, did you know Adam was in an accident last night?" Carol asked her son.

"No, I didn't. Is he okay?"

"Come with me. We're going to talk to Paige right now."

During the few minutes that it took to drive to Paige's home, Carol asked her son about the night before. She knew Adam had been at their home, but Carol had been out on a date and didn't really know what had gone on in her absence.

I heard them pull into the driveway and was waiting for her at the door. Carol gave me a hug and held me for a few seconds before letting go. I was thinking that was what I needed from Clay. I wanted him to hold me and tell me it was going to be okay and that he would be there for both of us.

"Let's sit in the breezeway. Could I get you some iced tea?"

"No, thank you."

"Billy told me Adam was at our house last night. He said Adam had too much to drink and Jenny didn't want to leave with him. After he called you, he left. Billy and one of his friends drove Jenny home. Billy hadn't heard from Adam today, so he assumed that he and Jenny had made up."

"Carol, do you know where they got the booze?" I asked.

Billy quickly said, "Uncle Don got it for us. He gets it for us all the time."

I wondered if Billy was always that truthful or if he just didn't want to be a party to someone losing his life. He looked frightened and sad that Adam was in such a grim situation. Adam and Billy had grown up like brothers. Carol and I had been pregnant at the same time, and our sons had been born one month apart. I had taken care of Billy when he was a baby while Carol worked, and he was like part of the family. The two boys had gone to school together and had remained friends for seventeen years.

"Carol, I have no idea where this will lead, but the attorney wants to know your brother's name. I wanted you to hear about this from me. I'm sure when the newspaper gets here there will be something in it about the accident, and I didn't want you to read about this in the paper. I appreciate you coming over, and I'll let you know what the attorney has to say."

"I can't tell you how sorry I am that this happened. If Don got the booze for the boys then he's is in trouble, too.

Tell Adam we're thinking about him. If there's anything that I can do, please let me know."

"I can't think of anything now. I appreciate you coming over."

Carol and Billy left. Carol knew I needed space and that Clay would be home soon.

Soon after they left I heard the thump of the paper hitting the house, I opened the front door and picked up the paper. On the front page I saw the headlines, *State Trooper Dies In Early Morning Chase.* I sank into a chair. It was all too real, and there was no escaping it. The newspaper had made it sound as though Adam was some crazed teenager. It was incomprehensible that my sweet and loving son could be the person I was reading about.

I started praying, "God, please give me the strength to see this awful accident through to the end. Please be with the Lather family. They, too, need strength. Wrap your loving arms around them and help them through these dark days. God, please watch over my son and help him to come through this a stronger person."

I heard Clay's truck pull into the driveway.

"Hi," Clay said trying to start a conversation, knowing I was probably still angry with him for not giving me the money I had asked for. "How did it go at the attorney's today? Did you find out what they are charging him with?"

"We really don't know yet. Jim said there is talk about them filing charges in Kokomo for running a stop light and if they charge him here and he pleads guilty, then they can't charge him with anything in Miami county. It doesn't make sense to me. I called Gordon and asked him to contact Daddy without Mama knowing what was going on and asked him to send me the retainer money. Gordon wired the money right away. I'll pay him back. You don't have to worry about any of this. I'll take care of Adam and his bills. I wouldn't want you to spend any of your precious deer hunting money."

Clay looked shocked. He never said a word, but he knew he had just been shut out of our lives.

The newspaper gave the name and address of Adam. I had thought that juveniles were protected. "I guess when you kill a state trooper being a juvenile doesn't matter."

My anguish was added to almost nightly with letters to the editor about the accident. This one was a double-edged sword.

## Get tough on drunks

*The time for leniency and forgiveness for drivers that drink is over. In less than a week in our area, the life of a friend and fellow police officer, Bob Lather, was snuffed out. Then two young lives were lost on Friday morning. Both accidents had alcohol involved. What a waste.*

*People raise all kinds of heck about gun control. What's the difference between an individual with a gun killing someone and an intoxicated individual driving a car killing someone?*

*We already have pretty tough gun laws, but the individual who wants a gun can still get one. Just like guns, we also have tough laws on alcohol: but if a minor wants liquor, there is always someone who will sell it to him or go and get it for him.*

*Where we need control is to make the penalty so severe that it will discourage a crime from* *happening. If you kill, either with a gun or a vehicle, the penalty should match the crime. If you are arrested for driving under the influence, regardless if you are an adult or a juvenile, it should be automatic year in jail, $1000.00 fine and loss of driving privileges for a year or more. If a life is taken, the penalty should be more severe.*

*We can't continue to be so lenient with the drunk driver. Fines of $50 or $100, or restricted or suspended driver licenses isn't the answer.*

*I don't want to listen to someone say we haven't got enough money in the budget to help investigate and prosecute the criminals. Is a budget over-extension worth a human life?*

*The bartender or liquor store clerk that sells liquor to an already intoxicated subject is guilty also. The person who purchases the liquor for a juvenile is another who helps pull the trigger.*

*The time for doing something to change the penalty for driving under the influence is now. Hound your lawmakers, your prosecutor, and your judges. Let's get the drunk driver off the road.*

I read another one; this one was in response to an earlier letter.

*The entertainment media did not give the youth the alcohol beverages or tell him to out-run the police officer. Also, I don't believe the boy had any thoughts of "The Dukes of Hazzard" or "Starsky and Hutch" the night of the police chase.*

*If we are to blame anyone we are to blame ourselves, for you and I, as well as everybody who lives in this society are the guilty ones. We let Mr. Lather down the night he died.*

*So what must we do to prevent, time and time again, the needless loss of human life and the scattered lives of everyone involved?*

*First, I agree the youth must be punished. His disregard for human life, as well as his own, must be punished to the full extent of the law.*

*Second, I agree the youth's accomplices, whoever he or she may be, must also be punished for contributing to a minor. They must be held accountable for the boy's actions.*

*Third, we must enact new laws and penalties on drunk drivers, laws so severe people would take warning when drinking not to get behind the wheel intoxicated.*

*Fourth, we must petition the state legislators to bring these laws into effect, to bring this slaughter off the roads.*

*Fifth, the persons involved in such accidents, as a judge or jury see fit must compensate the victims in such accidents.*

*Sixth, we must give police more power to get people off the roads.*

*Justice must be done but let's start where the malignancy begins, the drunk driver. To remember Robert J. Lather Jr., let's begin by writing our legislators and governor, asking them to pass desperately needed laws. Let's not have another youth kill another Robert Lather.*

Adam's accident was almost unbearable and never let up, day or night.  There was no place to escape the hurt I was feeling. Clay had been my best friend for so many years, yet now he was acting like a stranger. The accident was bad enough, but to feel like I was losing my husband, too, was causing double stress.  I felt like I couldn't share the responsibility of Adam with him. He had refused to give me the money, and I had remembered that I promised Clay when we were married that if things didn't work out for us I would never hold him responsible for Adam financially. Now it was time to keep the promise and not burden Clay with the responsibility.  Besides that, I was still angry with him, and as long as I stayed angry it would be easy to keep the promise.  Being angry gave me additional strength to fight for Adam and myself. As long as I kept that attitude I would be okay, or at least that was what I was telling myself.

The newspaper seemed to hold a grip on my daily activities; I couldn't wait to see what else would be reported in this one-sided story.

Didn't people ever wonder if the family of the perpetrator had feelings and was as hurt over the accident as the victim's family?  It seemed like the public's duty was to add to the heartache with its uninformed opinions.  Didn't the people who wrote to the newspaper in their *Letters to the Editor* ever wonder if they had enough information to write in and say, *Stretch him out in the road and run over him.* Or did they ever consider how they would feel if it were their son or grandson; or did they think they were immune to situations like I now found myself in.

"Ignorance," I said aloud. That's the only explanation I could give it. People who wrote in without all of the information about an accident had to be ignorant. No one raises his children to be involved in something like this. What were these people thinking when they wrote into the newspaper? I wanted to meet one of them face-to-face and tell him just how I felt.

Of course, there were people who knew Adam who wrote in to respond to the letters. Even the sheriff's wife in Peru told Adam's grandmother that Adam didn't belong in jail, and what a nice young man he was. He wasn't the kind of person who had been in and out of trouble. The sheriff's wife had seen lots of personalities and she knew Adam wasn't a mean young man who didn't care about others.

Over and over in my mind I would replay the events of that terrible July evening, desperately wishing there were some way I could reach back in time and alter the events. When troubled sleep did finally come it was often interrupted when I would suddenly awake in the middle of the night, the realization of Adam's tragedy again holding me in its chilly grasp. The worst parts were the uncertainty and helplessness to do anything about the situation. What would happen to Adam? Would he go to prison? He was only seventeen years old. The thought of my dear son behind bars gripped my heart like a massive fist and tears would come unbidden. I wanted to reach out to him, hold him, reassure him, tell him, as I did when he was little and would come sleepy-eyed to our bedroom, that it was all just a bad dream and he should go back to sleep in his own bed. But it was all too real.

As much as I loved my son, there was little I could do to help him, aside from lending moral support and providing him with good legal defense. How often in those tense, sad months did I wish he could be little again and that his life could take a different road that would avoid this horrible episode. I would find myself not paying attention, not replying sometimes when someone spoke directly to me. My mind, hurt and troubled, would be far away. Only someone who had gone through a similar thing could appreciate the full extent of my pain and anxiety.

My heart ached, too, for Clay. If only he would hold me and tell me it would be okay, or at least talk to me and try to work things out. Being in his arms had been a safe and secure place for me, and I wanted desperately to be there again. But Clay had going square dancing on his mind, and I felt like I had lost him. I was angry with him for buying Adam the car, but if he just would have said that we would see this accident through together, I would have forgiven him. I knew buying something for someone was his way of saying that he cared. I just needed to be held and to hear him say that he loved me.

We slept in the same bed but we each stayed on our own sides. Each of us were being careful not to touch one another. It was as though we were playing some kind of a game and the one who reached out would be the loser. We only spoke when we had to and each day we were drifting farther apart. I wondered if Clay hurt at all from this accident. He wasn't one to speak of his feelings. He just kept busy and no one ever knew how he felt about anything.

The phone rang.

"Hello."

"Hi. I suppose you saw the letters to the editor in the newspaper tonight?" Carol asked.

"Yes, I did. They really upset me. I can't believe people can be so cruel. Or have so much time on their hands that all they have to do is write letters to the editor?"

"That's not really the reason I called you. Naturally I thought of you when I read the paper. But what I called to tell you is a friend of mine has a friend who's a state trooper and he told her that he thought Adam wouldn't get any jail time out of this because Lather pulled out in front of Adam. I thought it might make you feel better to know that it wasn't all Adam's fault," Carol said.

"The night of the accident when I went in to call the attorney I heard one of the officers telling someone on the phone that, 'He made a mistake and pulled out in front of someone.' I'll bet that's what he was talking about. I'll mention it to Adam's attorney. Keep your ears open we need all the help we can get. I really appreciate your friendship, Carol, and the way you have stood by us. Thanks for calling."


The next morning I called Jim's office and told him what Carol had told me.

"There are all kinds or rumors that get started when something like this happens. We could have a reconstruction of the accident done and that should tell us something." Jim said.

"How do I go about having that done?" I asked.

"I'll take care of it for you. I know a man who does reconstruction. I'll call him and we'll get on it right away."

"What about the witnesses? Have you talked to any of them?"

"I guess there is only one witness. I'll get a report of his testimony," Jim said.

"I thought you said there were several witnesses?"

"I'm told there is only one."

"Thank you, Jim."

I wondered what had happened to the *several witnesses* they said they had in the beginning?

Satisfied that I had done all I could at the time, I went back to selling real estate and worked at it night and day to keep myself from thinking. I hoped to be able to stay ahead of the attorney's bill.

Brian had become especially attentive to me and I found myself talking to him about Adam and my faltering marriage. He tried to help me with leads so I could stay ahead of the expenses. There were civil law suits filed and I had to pay two attorneys now. Jerry Angel had taken our lawsuits on, one for a million dollars and the other for one hundred and fifty thousand dollars. Mrs. Lather's attorney had filed against our homeowner's insurance policy and was trying to collect under "negligent entrustment." I couldn't think about the lawsuits. I trusted Jerry Angel to do what was in my best interest. Just trying to keep Adam's spirits up and act normal when I talked to my mother was about all I could handle in addition to work. Thinking about Clay was so painful I found myself crying every time I thought about him. I loved his big build and his fuzzy chest. I thought of all the intimate times we had together and how much I had learned to love him through the years.  Now it was like he was a different person.

# Chapter 4

It was August 21, and it was our eighteenth wedding anniversary. Clay came home from work and took a bath immediately. When I came in he had just finished dressing.

"Hello. Thought we would go out for dinner this evening, if that's okay with you?" he asked. I thought how he sounded like John Wayne when he said, "Hello."

"I suppose it is. I hadn't planned anything for this evening," I answered, thinking all the time that I didn't feel like celebrating an anniversary on a faltering marriage. I didn't say that, I kept my feelings to myself, thinking Clay didn't want to hear it if it didn't concern square dancing or deer hunting, or have something to do with one of the cars he was always working on in the garage. I freshened up and we left for our anniversary dinner.

We were led to a back table in the steak house. The lights were low and a candle was burning on each table. Normally I loved eating at the Colorado Steak House. I thought how romantic the restaurant looked, but how deceiving the two of us were. Supposedly celebrating eighteen years of marriage, we only spoke to each other when we had to. There was nothing on the menu that looked good to me. Clay had decided on steak, so I ordered a small filet. We sat in the restaurant across the table from one another like total strangers. In fact, strangers would've talked more, trying to get to know one another. After eighteen years we knew enough about one another to know that something was badly wrong with our marriage.

"What are you thinking about?" Clay asked.

"I don't know. I guess I was just wishing Adam were out of jail," I answered.

"Can't you forget about that for just one evening. He'll be out in a few more days. Just try to enjoy yourself tonight," he said gruffly.

I didn't say any more. I probably should have told him how hypocritical I felt celebrating eighteen years of marriage when we had been at one another's throats like we had been, but my mind wasn't into trying to work out our problems.

"No, I can't think of anything else. You won't talk to me about Adam and this situation, and I get more attention from Brian at work than I get from you. I am so sick of being the last person or thing on your list to give attention to. I need someone to hold me and comfort me, I don't need someone to tell me what to think, and what to feel, and when and how to feel it."

The waitress had brought our food and I choked down about half of my meal and felt the anger burning in my stomach. The attempt that Clay had made to have a nice anniversary dinner wasn't working for me. I really didn't understand how men think. Clay didn't support Adam or me, yet he seemed to think I would have a good time going out to dinner with him. I don't know about other women, but I have a real problem having fun with a man when I have a problem as large as this one is.

Adam remained in jail from July 6 to August 23 before the courts and attorneys could come up with appropriate bail. When they did, it wasn't a normal bail. This one made us totally responsible for Adam financially, but they would try him as an adult. What that meant to Clay and me was that if they put up $3,000 and Adam ran away, we had to pay the courts $30,000. The fact that we had just spent most of our money on remodeling our home was putting enough stress on us. I had borrowed money for the attorney; now I needed to come up with more money for the courts. I was confused. I couldn't see how the court could have Adam stand trial as an adult, yet have the parents responsible for all of the financial obligations. Relenting, Clay put in the money for Adam's bail out of his hunting money. I was beginning to think that he had second thoughts about his initial stance on helping Adam. Now he was being the person I had thought he was all along.

"I want this money back before I go deer hunting," Clay said, as he handed me the cash.

"Thank you, Clay, for loaning it to me. I'll do my best to have it back to you before hunting season."

I was wondering all the time how he could be so wrapped up in going deer hunting when we had this accident hanging over our heads. It was more than I could understand, but instead of fighting with Clay I promised to get his money back to him before his precious deer hunting trip.

Adam was released from jail a few days before school started. It was still hot, but the leaves on the trees were starting to turn and the sky was a brilliant blue. Adam was happy to be out of jail; however, he seemed much too quiet and preoccupied with his thoughts. He spent most of his time in his room or talking to his girlfriend Jenny on the phone.

The first day of school arrived and I was looking forward to Adam getting out of the house and focusing on something besides the accident. I went upstairs to wake him.

"Time to get up."

"Mom, I don't want to go to school."

"Adam, this is the first day of your senior year. I know it isn't going to be easy, but it will do you good to get back into school with your friends. I'll take you to school this morning. It's going to be all right. I promise."

"I don't want to go back to school. I can't concentrate. All I can think about is the accident. It's making me crazy."

"Give it a chance, Adam. After you get to school, you'll have other things to think about. Jenny is going to be waiting for you."

It was a cool morning and the leaves were putting on their brilliant colors for the coming fall. It felt good to have my son home and getting back to as normal a lifestyle as possible. When I dropped Adam off at school Jenny was waiting for him so they could walk to class together. I waved to Jenny and silently thanked God that she was there for Adam. Jenny and I had become friends after the accident. It was obvious that Jenny was fond of Adam. She had gone to see him regularly while he was in jail.

While the accident had brought Jenny and me closer, it had driven Clay and I further apart. Our marriage was under tremendous pressure day and night. There didn't seem to be a place to escape what was happening. Clay and I hardly spoke to one another. There was so much anger in both of us it was hard for either of us to function. I had begged Clay not to buy the car for Adam. Clay probably saw it as a generous gesture, but all I could think of was that the accident wouldn't have happened if Clay hadn't have bought the car. That was just like Clay to buy something for someone instead of telling him that he loved him. We were going our separate ways. Clay didn't miss a square dance, and I would work as long as I could before I would come home.

After the first week of classes it was obvious that sending Adam to school wasn't helping him at all. He couldn't concentrate and thought of nothing but the accident. I relayed this information to Adam's caseworker and the courts suggested a mental evaluation for Adam.

When the day of the appointment arrived, I hurried home to pick Adam up. "I hope going to see this doctor will help you, Adam. You seem so sad, and I'm really worried about you." Adam just looked at me and never responded.

The doctor had us fill out a lengthy questionnaire and asked for additional information. "I want to put Adam on some medication. He is in a delicate frame of mind. It will take a few days to evaluate these tests and then I'll know more how to treat Adam. Make an appointment to come and see me on Friday and we'll talk then," Dr. Miller said.

"Thanks for your help. I'll see you on Friday," I said as Adam and I got up and left the room.

"Mom, I can't go back to school. I can't concentrate. I'm making bad grades. Most of the kids don't talk to me. I see them pointing and whispering. I can't take it any more. Please don't make me go back."

"All right, Adam, you can stay home until we get the results back from your test. Then we'll ask the doctor what he thinks about you continuing. I just want what's best for you, honey. I know you would never harm a flea and this accident has been overwhelming for you."

Adam spent most of his time in his bedroom, holding little toys that he had saved since he was very young, as if they would turn him back into the bright, happy, little boy he had been. He seldom smiled and spent time on the phone talking to Jenny after she came home from school.

On Friday, I was early for my appointment with Dr. Miller. I sat in the waiting room reading the latest copy of *Better Homes and Gardens* and imagined myself in one of the beautiful garden pictures. It had been a dream of mine to have a beautiful garden that I could sit and read in. I had it pictured in my mind, a wicker swing, hanging from a large oak tree nestled under flowering wisteria. There would be dogwood trees, and azalea blooming under an ancient oak tree draped with Spanish moss. Of course, my mental picture was in the South and I was living in Indiana and the magnificent Oak in my mind only grows in the South.

"Mrs. Mitchell, the doctor will see you now."

I felt the peace of the garden leaving me as I walked into Dr. Miller's office.

"Good afternoon, Mrs. Mitchell, I appreciate you coming in to see me without your son. I have carefully gone over the test, and I would like to recommend that Adam be put in the Stress Center in Indianapolis. The test indicates that he is escaping reality and if we don't get him some help we could lose him completely. Let me show you a graph of his emotional state."

The doctor continued explaining what was going on with Adam's emotions. "He is in worse shape than I had anticipated. I think we should get him to the hospital immediately. He could become suicidal. I've called St.

Vincent and they have room for him. Could you take him down there today?"

"I suppose I can. What will they do to him there?"

"They'll medicate him so he can get some rest. It's going to take some time and treatment, but I think he will be all right. Adam can't accept that this accident has happened. We have to help him deal with reality. They are really good at St. Vincent's. He'll be in good hands. I'll call them and tell them to be expecting Adam. Also, Mrs. Mitchell, I think it would be a good idea if you and your husband take the test, too. That way I'll have a better understanding of your home life and it'll help me with Adam's treatment. Take these with you and get them back to me as soon as you can." Dr. Miller handed me two sets of papers for me and for Clay to fill out.

I thanked the doctor and rushed home to find Adam. He was in his room sitting on the bed holding a small stuffed tiger. He had had that Tiger since he was an infant. His stereo was on low and he didn't seem to hear me enter the room.

"Adam." He looked up at me with tears in his eyes.

"Oh, Honey, what's wrong?"

"I don't know, Mom. I just feel so sad and unhappy. I've never felt this way before I..." The tears were running down his face.

"Come on, Adam, help me get some of your clothes together. The doctor thinks you need to be in the hospital, and I agree with him. He wants me to take you to St. Vincent in Indianapolis. They're are going to try to help you get through this. We'll make it together. I'll always be there for you." I was holding him and wishing I could take away all of his sadness. Adam just stood there while I tried to get together the things he might want during his stay in the hospital.

I left a note for Clay, and the two of us left for Indianapolis. Adam was silent all the way. I felt bad that he was going to be away from home again, but I knew he needed more help than I could give him in order to learn to cope with his emotional problems.

The next day I phoned Adam's attorney.

"May I speak to Jim Fleming, please?"

"Just one minute. I'll put you on hold and he'll be right with you."

"Hi, Jim, this is Paige Mitchell. I thought I should tell you that the court-appointed psychiatrist has admitted Adam to the Stress Center in Indianapolis. I took him down there yesterday and it was too late to call you when I got home."

"That's good that they're getting Adam some help. I'm glad you called. I have the reconstruction of the accident report. According to the pros, Adam did everything he could do to avoid hitting the trooper. The report states that Adam had a split second to make a decision. He pulled to the left to avoid hitting the trooper, and the trooper pulled to the left to get out of Adam's way, putting him directly in front of Adam. I'm not sure that this will help our case. We still have the high speed and alcohol to deal with," Jim said.

"I know. It sounds pretty hopeless, doesn't it?"

"Let's think positive. Maybe we can get him off with probation. I'll get back to you as soon as I know something."

# **Chapter 5**

Two days later when I pulled into the driveway, Clay had arrived home before me. I picked the mail up from the table. Shuffling though it, I found an opened letter from the attorney. Opening it quickly I read. "The trial date has been set for October, 12th 1982."

"Hi," Clay said.

"Did you see the date that has been set for the hearing?" I asked.

"Yes, I did." He said this very self-assuredly. "I told you I want my money to go deer hunting. I'm not letting this stop my life. I'm going to go hunting. I don't know how you're going to get my money back before the trial, but I want that money."

"I'll get your money, Clay. I just can't believe the date is at the same time as your deer-hunting trip. I also can't believe you would let Adam go to this hearing without you while you go all the way to Colorado to go deer hunting. Talk about having your priorities screwed up. You buy the kid a car and then turn your back on him when he gets into trouble with it. Well, you go deer hunting. We'll do just fine without you." I could feel the anger come back instantly. My stomach was burning like fire.

"You might like to know that the doctor thinks you and I need to be evaluated, too. He said he cannot treat Adam without knowing what is going on in this home. I brought home some papers for you to fill out. I'll lay them on your desk. I'd like to return them to the doctor tomorrow. That won't interfere with anything you have planned, will it?"

I was seething. I went outside and started raking the few leaves that had fallen and then picking the last of the tomatoes from my garden. Thank God for my garden and having a lawn to rake. It made me feel better and right then I needed to feel better. I stayed as busy as possible until late into the evening so that I would be so tired I would drop when I went to bed. It seemed like the only formula for me to get any sleep.

I had my test completed and I returned both of the tests to the doctor's secretary. I asked, "When will the evaluations be complete?"

"I'll make you an appointment for the first of next week. I'm sure that Dr. Miller will have them ready by then."

I couldn't visit Adam for the first week that he was in the hospital, and I was anxious to see if he was feeling any better. I drove alone to Indianapolis. I never asked Clay if he wanted to go with me. Our anger with one another seemed to flare up more on a daily basis, as though we were throwing gasoline on it.

Adam was happy to see me and had a slight smile on his face. It appeared that he had adjusted as well as he could to the routine at the hospital. He looked a little glassy eyed, but I thought it was better to have him on medication than in the mental turmoil he had been in. I could only stay for an hour, and we talked mostly about the activities at the hospital. It was difficult to tell after talking to him for a while if he was accepting reality or if the medicine had him numbed. My gut was telling me his reality was being at the hospital, and the medication was just giving his mind a rest from the turmoil he had been in. I never mentioned the accident. I wanted Adam to come back to the person he had been before the accident.

# **Chapter 6**

I heard Clay getting up early. It was the day he would leave to go deer hunting in Colorado. I wanted to be going with him. We'd had many good deer hunting trips together, experiencing new adventures like a couple of buddies. One trip in particular came to mind.

We had driven to Montrose, Colorado and set up camp. On opening morning we left camp before sunrise to get into a good position before hunting season opened at daybreak. We drove into a clearing to park the truck just as the sun broke on the horizon. Clay immediately saw three deer on the hillside. He got out of his truck and leaned onto the hood to steady his rifle. The deer were quite a ways off. He slowly found them in his scope and looked for the largest one. With one slow pull on the trigger he watched as the deer fell. The two of us ran toward the animal, and together we dragged, pushed and loaded it into the bed of the truck.

"Clay, you stay here with the deer. I paid for a license and I'm going over the ridge and find one for me," I said.

"Are you sure you want to go into the woods by yourself?"

"It's not a problem. I use to play in the woods all the time as a child. I'll be back."

"Don't get lost, and don't go too far."

With the rifle slung over my shoulder, I began my climb over the big ridge. Clay stayed with his trophy, showing it off to anyone who happened to pass by. Clay listened to each shot and wondered if it was me who was doing the shooting. He knew I was a good shot, and if a deer came within sight I would down him. Several hours passed before he heard someone shouting. Looking over the western slope of the ridge he thought he saw some movement. Using the scope on his rifle he carefully checked the ridge. That's when he spotted his wife dragging a dead animal. He drove his truck to the far end at the foot of the ridge and started walking up the steep terrain to help me. I saw Clay working his way up the ridge at a diagonal climb. When I thought he was in hearing distance I shouted.

"I got a eight point buck."

Silence.

"Did you hear me? I said I got an eight point buck," I shouted again.

"I heard you the first time," he shouted back.

As he climbed closer to help me I wondered what was going on in his mind. *I'll bet he's started wondering what it's going to be like when we get home and he has to tell his hunting buddies that his wife got a bigger buck than he did.*

When he was close enough to see the deer he smiled and said, "I thought you said it had eight points!"

"I did say that. I was just wondering if you knew how it felt to be outdone," I answered. He looked up and smiled at me and I could feel the love between us. Clay had never talked much, but when he gave me one of those smiles, it said volumes about how he felt, and I knew I was in good standing with him.

Clay came into the bedroom and softly said.

"Are you awake?"

I pretended to be sleeping. I didn't want to have to say goodbye to Clay. I was angry with him, yet didn't want him to leave. Clay turned and left for his annual Colorado hunting trip.

It would be two more days before the hearing. It was like a countdown to doom. I tried to stay busy, cleaning the house and wiping away the tears every two seconds. How could Clay leave me when I needed him so much right now? I called my parents in Georgia.

"Hi, Daddy. How's Mama doing?"

"Your mother's doing pretty fair. She keeps asking where you are and saying Paige said she was coming home to take care of me."

"Daddy, the hearing is in two days. Adam's still in the hospital. The attorney seems to think they will leave him in the hospital until the doctor releases him. I have to pick him up for the hearing. I can be packed and ready to come home for a few days after I take Adam back to the hospital. Do you think that Mama seeing me will help her?"

"I think it would make her happy to see you, Paige."

"Okay, Daddy, I'll make arrangements to come home for a few days after the hearing is over. At least then I can tell Mama what has been going on. We should know what's going to happen to Adam by that time."

"I'll call and let you know when I'll be there and I'll tell Mama what's been going on when I get there. If she knows I'm all right and Adam is in the hospital and not the jail, she might take it better. I'll see you in a few days. "Could I talk to Mama for a minute?"

"Sure, here she is."

"Hi, Mama."

"Where are you?" The words were muffled and didn't sound like my Mama.

"I'm in Indiana, Mama, but I'm coming home to see you."

"I'm so glad. When will you be here?"

"I told Daddy I'll call and let you know, but in just a few days. Are you doing okay?'

"I still can't move my left side and they have to help me do everything. I can't seem to do anything by myself. I'm such a burden for your Daddy and Dorothy."

"Mama, you're not a burden. We all love you and want to help you get better. Put Daddy back on the phone. You let them help you while you need help. You've helped us all of our lives, so now let us help you, okay? I love you, Mama, and I'll see you in a couple of days."

"Hi."

"Daddy, she still sounds funny."

"I know. We have good days and bad days."

"Daddy, I love you both and I'll see you in a couple of days. Bye."

I had an appointment with the psychiatrist to get the results from the evaluation. I was eager to hear what the doctor had to say.

"Good afternoon, Mrs. Mitchell. Adam tells me you came to see him on Sunday. I think we are making some progress, but I intend to keep him on medication until the trial is over. He's eating better now and that's a good sign."

"I could tell he was heavily sedated. He usually has more life to him than what I saw. Tell me, how did the test come out?"

"To be honest with you, I couldn't believe it. I've never seen these results on a psychological evaluation before. Your husband's were so low they were off the scale. The test looked like it had been given to a pet rock. He shows no emotions at all. On the other end, Adam was off the scale in the other direction. It is unbelievable that these two extremes are in the same household. You were the most normal. However, you were out of the normal range in two areas. One, you're more feminine than normal, and two, you have a tendency to repress your emotions. Counseling would benefit your family."

"We were in counseling when this accident happened. Adam had run away from home in April. I told Clay and Adam then that the only way I could continue to live in the same house with them was to get some professional help. According to the counselor we were seeing, the two of them were using me for a battlefield. I was going nuts. There wasn't any peace in our home. The counselor suggested that Clay and Adam do something together and leave me out of it. They planned a trip to Michigan for a car show. Right after they left, I got a call that my mother had suffered a stroke and they didn't know if she would live or not. I left for Georgia, and when they were due back, I called home and told Clay what had happened. I don't think he believed me since his response was 'I knew you would go to Georgia the minute I turned my back.'

"He never asked how my mother was doing. All he wanted to know was when I was going to come home. I stayed with my mother for one week, and I came home on Saturday. This accident happened on Monday. My mother is out of the hospital now, but she keeps asking my dad why I haven't come back home to help care for her. I told her when she was in the hospital that when she got out I would be back. She doesn't know about the accident yet."

"Paige, try to keep your family in counseling. It's the only way to get through this. I'll contact you with a progress report on Adam, and you and your husband need to continue seeing a counselor. Thanks for coming in, and good luck."

I had wondered why Clay didn't cry at his father's funeral. In fact, I had wondered about him a lot in our later years of marriage. Talking to him was like talking to a brick wall. He would look at me with a blank expression, as though he couldn't understand anyone feeling the way I did. At least Dr. Miller had clarified one thing for me: Clay had no emotions, or rather they were buried so deep that I couldn't get to them.

The morning came for me to drive to Indianapolis to pick up Adam at St. Vincent's hospital. He was ready and waiting for me when I got there.

"Hi, Mom." He gave me a big hug. "Well, this is the day we've been waiting for. I know I can cope with this better when I know what the future holds for me. It's the *not knowing* that drives me nuts."

"Just keep praying and we'll get though this together," I said.

"Mom, I can't believe Dad went to Colorado while this hearing is going on."

"I can't understand him doing it either. Lord knows, if we ever needed him, we need him now. But we're both strong, and we'll get through this together no matter what. I called my Dad and told him that when I bring you back to the hospital this afternoon that I would be taking a plane to Georgia. I'm sure they are going to keep you in the hospital for a while. I'll be back here in a week. I'm afraid if someone else besides me tells Mama about your situation, she might not take it well. I thought if I told her myself, I could be there and see how she takes it. I hope you understand."

"No problem, Mom. I just hope Grandma will be okay. Be sure and tell her I love her and not to worry about me. I'll be all right." I noticed a slight smile. Maybe being in the hospital was helping after all.

We arrived in Peru a little early. The Courthouse was a three-story building with two huge stone pillars flanking each side of the entry. The top and bottom story had rectangular windows and the second story's windows were arched at the top with keystones at the top of each window. It was a beautiful structure. As we entered the building I noticed that the center of the courthouse was open to the third floor and had an extremely large American flag hanging in the center space and at the very top was a stained glass sky light. Adam and I started climbing the white marble stairs that provided handrails of oak a top of some of the prettiest wrought iron work I had ever seen. It reminded me of Savannah. A lot of the homes in the historical district in Savannah have wrought iron railings. When we were on the third floor we both looked over the railing and noticed the Preamble framed more than one full story high, hanging on the wall of the second story.

Shortly, Adam's attorney rounded the corner and came over to where we were standing.

"Hi. Did you just get here?"

"We've been here for a few minutes. Jim, did you hear about the Atwell case in Indianapolis?" I asked. Not giving Jim a chance to respond, I continued. "I believe the police *forgot* to give him a blood alcohol test. When they remembered the next morning his alcohol level was .16. He was put on probation and doesn't have to serve any time."

"I know about that case, but we can't compare that case to this one," Jim said.

"I don't know why you can't compare the cases. He was a policeman, and should have known better. Those two teenagers he hit and killed on a sidewalk aren't any less dead than the state trooper," I argued.

"Look, Paige, what we have here is political. The prosecutor is going out of office at the end of the year, and they say the new one is one mean son-of-a-gun. Adam stands a better chance with Judge Embrey and this prosecutor. We need to dispose of this today. If we postpone, there's a good chance that we can't get back on the docket until after the first of the year."

"Can we get a change of venue to another county?" I asked.

"Wouldn't do us any good. He was a state trooper. Adam's going to get punishment no matter where we go. We're better off here."

Adam interrupted, "Mom, let's just get this over with. I can't take any postponement. I need to know what they are going to do to me!"

I reached out for my son's hand and gave it a squeeze. "Are you sure you just want to get it over with?"

"Yes, please, Mom, just get it over with."

"Okay, let's get on with it."

# **Chapter 7**

The three of us entered the courtroom through the tall oak doors that had "Miami Superior Court" painted on the glass in gold paint. I noticed Brian sitting with Pastor Rendelman from our church. I nodded and took a seat behind Adam and his attorney. I knew the people to my left had to be the family of Trooper Lather. And the rest of the courtroom, on that side of the room, was filled with men in uniform. They must have arrived early and parked on a different side of the courthouse than we had. The room had a feeling much like I would imagine a gas chamber has before someone is put to death.

The Bailiff started with, "Be it remembered on the12th day of October, 1982, the same being calendar year 1982, the State of Indiana, vs. Adam A. Mitchell, the foregoing cause of action came to be heard before the Honorable Bruce C. Embrey, sole Judge of the Miami Superior Court."

I knew the 12th day of October, 1982 would always be an important date to remember. In fact, it would be hard to forget. Adam looked pale and frightened sitting next to his attorney and I couldn't have looked much different. It would have been easier if Clay were there to hold my hand and tell me it was going to be okay. But Clay wasn't there.

"This is cause number J-62-82, in the matter of Adam A. Mitchell, a child under the age of 18 years. Mr. Fleming, you're representing Mr. Mitchell?" Judge Embrey asked.

"Yes, sir."

"And he is here with his parents?"

"His mother is here."

"The State of Indiana is represented by James H. Grund, Prosecuting Attorney. We're here pursuant to the State's motion to waive juvenile jurisdiction pursuant to Indiana Code 31-6-2-4. Mr. Grund, are you ready to proceed on your motion?

"Yes, your Honor." Mr. Grund answered.

"If I'm understanding the waiver statue correctly, this is a mandatory wavier under the provisions of Paragraph D of 31-6-2-4, and it states 'the court shall waive, upon motion of the prosecutor and full investigation and hearings, if it finds 1) that the child is charged with an act that, if committed by an adult, would, and then under paragraph C reckless homicide, a Class C Felony under IC 35-42-1-5. That is, in fact the charge. 2) There is a probable cause to believe that the child has committed the act, and 3) the child was sixteen years of age or older when the act was allegedly committed, unless it would be in the best interest of the child, and the safety and welfare of the community for him to remain within the Juvenile Justice System.' It would seem to me, under that statue then, that the State must prove probable cause, and the age of the child, and that the burden is then on the Defense to show whether it is in the best interest of the child and the safety and welfare of the community for him to remain in the Juvenile system. Is that the way both counsels are interpreting the statute?"

"Yes, your Honor." Mr. Grund answered. The Court should note, however, there are two other charges, which I essentially would consider to be lesser-included offenses. With reckless homicide, should it be waived, we would consider the other two to be waived also. However, we would not intend to proceed to trial with regard to the other two charges."

"All right, we're under a different statute for the waiver of the other two charges. The court may waiver, if it finds…that would require a repetitive pattern of conduct or heinous crime, and we're looking at Driving While Intoxicated and Resisting Law Enforcement as the others."

"Causing death while Driving While Intoxicated," interrupted Mr. Grund.

"Is that one of the juvenile charges?" the Judge asked.

It appeared to me that none of the players knew exactly what they where doing here.

"Yes. What I'm saying is they all three grow out of the same offense. It would seem somewhat unrealistic to waive one and leave two in Juvenile Court," said Grund.

"All right, well, the primary charge…yeah, in lesser offenses it would, I would think, be waived. If you're not going to proceed on the other two in Adult Court, in the event that there's a wavier, I don't see that we really have a problem."

"No, I don't either, but I was just making that clear for the purposes of the record."

"Okay. Very good. You may proceed, Mr. Grund."

"Call Kenneth Roland."

"Officer Roland, would you raise your right hand, please?"

Kenneth F. Roland, being first duly sworn to tell the truth, the whole truth and nothing but the truth, testified as follows:

"Would you state your name and occupation, please?"

"Kenneth F. Roland, Detective with the Indiana State Police."

"Detective Roland, did you know Robert J. Lather?"

"Yes, sir, I did."

"And how long did you know him?"

"Approximately eight years. Seven and a half to eight years."

"And prior to his death, what was his occupation?"

"He was a state trooper with the Indiana State Police."

"And did you have occasion to investigate the circumstances surrounding his death, occurring on July the 6th, 1982?"

"Yes, sir, I did."

"In the course of the investigation did you come to know Adam A. Mitchell?"

"Yes, sir, I did."

"Is he present in court today?"

"Yes, sir, he is. He's sitting next to defense counsel at the other table."

"Let the records show the witness has identified the Respondent," the Judge interjected.

"Would you briefly state to the Court how you became involved in this investigation?"

"Okay. On July the 6th, 1982, I was notified at home that Trooper Lather had been killed in an automobile accident, and I was requested by personnel at the Post to come to the Post to start interviewing witnesses, and I was also told they had the suspect there at the post, administering a breathalyzer test at that time."

*He's saying there were witnesses. What's going on here?* I wondered.

"Now, in the course of your investigation, did you find where this accident had occurred?"

"Yes, sir, I did."

"And where was that?"

"It was on U.S. 31 in Miami County, approximately just north of 800 County Road South on 31 in the northbound lane."

"In the course of interviewing other officers involved in the accident, did you find what the Respondent, Adam Mitchell, had been doing immediately prior to the accident?"

"Yes, sir."

"And would you state for the court what that was?"

"Howard County officers noticed the vehicle in which Mr. Mitchell was driving ran a red light at Markland and U.S. 31 in Kokomo, at which time officers gave pursuit. A short time later he passed another Howard County Deputy at a high rate of speed and ran another red light. At that time, that officer gave pursuit and they proceeded on U.S. 31 from Howard County into Miami County."

"And, did they state to you any approximate rates of speed during that chase?"

"They stated it was in excess of ninety miles an hour."

"And what happened then, after the chase got into Miami County?"

"They notified their dispatcher to notify the State Police Post to see if it had any officers in the vicinity to give assistance, in reference to their pursuits. At that time Trooper Lather had just left the Peru area and was southbound on U. S. 31. They notified him of the pursuit, in which he indicated that he was down in the vicinity of 500 South."

"He would have been southbound at the time?"

"He was southbound, yes, sir. The last transmission they had was he was in the…near Hal-Dar's, and that was the last conversation they had with him on the radio."

I wondered why he changed what he was saying.

"Did you take a statement, then, from Charles P. Wink?"

"Yes, sir, I did."

"And did Mr. Wink, at any time that evening, have occasion to see Trooper Lather's car?"

"Yes, sir, he did."

"Would you tell the Court what Mr. Wink stated to you in regard to what he saw of Trooper Lather's car?"

"Mr. Wink was northbound on U.S. 31, and he noticed a vehicle that was making a turn in the crossover by Hal-Dar's from the southbound into the northbound lane. Wink stated that he happened to look up into his rearview mirror at the time to see if he was going to have to change lanes if it was going to be clear, at which time he stated he saw some headlights at a great distance back. He stated that the car made the U-turn and was driving in the left-hand lane, the passing lane, and it stayed there the whole time. A short time later, the car turned on its red lights, overhead red lights, it was approximately the same time that…"

"Is that the first he realized it was a Trooper's car, then?"

"Yes, sir. Approximately about the same time this vehicle passed Mr. Wink at a high rate of speed, in excess, again of approximately ninety miles an hour. It passed his vehicle at that time and proceeded in the passing lane. He stated he never saw any brake lights, and then he ran into the back of the Trooper's car."

"Okay, at the time the second vehicle ran into the back of the Trooper's car, were the Trooper's lights…flashing lights, strobe lights and so forth on?"

"Yes, sir, they were."

"And, according to Mr. Wink, did the Trooper's car ever change lanes after entering the passing lane?"

"No, sir. He stated that the Trooper's car stayed in the passing lane at all times."

"And did Mr. Wink indicate whether the second car that passed him ever changed lanes?"

"No, sir, it did not. It stayed in the passing lane also until the time of the collision."

"Prior to the time of the collision, did Mr. Wink indicate whether or not he saw any break lights come on, on the second car?"

"He stated he didn't see any break lights at all."

"Do you know Trooper Kenneth Baker?

"Yes, sir, I do."

"How do you know him?"

"Trooper Baker is assigned out of the Peru Post also, the same Post that I am assigned out of. I've worked with Trooper Baker for approximately eight years."

"Does he have any specialties?"

"Yes, sir, he's an accident Reconstructionist."

"And did he reconstruct the events leading up to this accident?"

"Yes, sir."

"Were his findings as a result of the accident reconstruction substantially in concurrence with the evidence that you found by taking Mr. Wink's statements and the statements of the other police officers involved?"

"Yes, sir, they were."

"Okay, is it correct that his findings were that Trooper Lather's car, just immediately prior to the accident, was headed at a small angle toward the brem at the left side of the road?"

"Yes, sir."

"And, likewise, I believe, the second car which you later found to be driven by Adam Mitchell, was also headed at a slight angle toward the median or left side of the road?"

"Yes, sir"

"And was it then reported to you who was the driver of the second vehicle?"

"I can't think of his name. He's with the Howard County Sheriff's Department. One of the officers was Officer Goodnight. The other one was Jerry Evans. The officer who went up to the car and got Mr. Mitchell out of the car was Jerry Evans, with the Howard County Sheriff's Department."

"So, it was reported that Adam Mitchell was the driver of the second vehicle?"

"Yes, sir."

"And did you interview Adam Mitchell on this particular night?"

"No, sir, I did not."

"Do you know whether or not there was any blood alcohol test or breathalyzer test taken on that night?"

"Yes, sir, both tests were taken."

"And do you know what the results of the breathalyzer exam was?"

"Yes, sir. It was .12% blood alcohol."

"Do you know approximately what time that was taken?"

"I believe it was approximately two-thirty. Two-thirty or quarter to three, somewhere right around there. Just as I got to the Post they were taking the test at that time."

"And was there, later, a blood sample withdrawn and sent to the State Police Lab for analysis?"

"Yes, sir."

"What time was the blood sample withdrawn?"

"Again, I believe it was 4:35 a.m."

"Do you know what the results of the analysis of the blood sample was?"

"Yes, sir, it was .11% blood alcohol."

"And that was taken approximately two hours after the breathalyzer?"

"Yes, sir."

"And the events that you've described as they relate to Miami County occurred on U. S. 31, which is a public highway in Miami County, Indiana?"

"Yes, sir."

"I have no further questions."

"Mr. Fleming," the judge said as Adam's attorney rose from his chair.

"Was the blood also examined for the presence of dangerous drugs?"

"Yes, sir, it was."

"And did you receive a report back from Dr. Forney at the State Laboratory?"

"Yes, sir, I did."

"Did it indicate that there was the presence of any drugs in the blood sample from Mr. Mitchell?"

"There were no traces of any drugs in the blood."

"And for our record, .12% blood alcohol. What is the legal limit in Indiana?"

"Point 10 percent."

"That's all."

"Any re-direct, Mr. Grund?" the Judge asked.

"No, your Honor."

"You may step down. Does the state have any other witnesses?"

"Call Diana Monaghan," Mr. Grund said.

Diane Monaghan stood and made her way to the witness box on the right side of the judge. She looked almost as scared as Adam. Diane was an attractive lady in a neat and orderly sort of way. Her sandy blonde hair was always combed and she had a reserved way about her. She had been very friendly and sympathetic when she came to our home for our case study, but there was the air about her that said, *I can't get too close.*

"Diane Monaghan, being first sworn to tell the truth, the whole truth, and nothing but the truth."

"I do."

"Would you state your name and occupation, please?"

"Diana Monaghan, probation Officer of Miami County."

"Miss Monaghan, in the course of your duties as Probation Officer, have you come to know Adam A. Mitchell?"

"Yes, I have."

"Did you, in fact, do a…I don't even know what you call them…a Pre-Filing Home Study?"

"Yes, I did."

"At that time, did you determine what Adam's age was?

"At the time of preliminary, he was seventeen."

"And what is his birth date?"

"Mid-September. This past September he turned eighteen."

"Okay, would September the 15th, 1964, refresh your recollection?"

"That's correct, uh-huh."

"So, at the time that you did your study, he was seventeen. At the present time he is eighteen, then?"

"That's correct."

"Did you make attempts to find a placement for him, during the time that he was in the Miami County Jail, at some type of a juvenile facility?"

"Yes, I did."

"What type of a facility were you looking for?"

"I originally checked with the Adolescent Unit at LaRue D. Carter Hospital in Indianapolis. The parents had made original contact with La Rue Carter and Dr. McAfee felt that this might be appropriate, so I went ahead and prepared the work. In talking with Dr. McAfee, and in talking about Adam, he thought possible the University Psychiatric Center would be more feasible. The University Psychiatric Center deals with patients who have emotional illness that may be complicated by physical problems, which we thought may have been some of Adam's problems at that time, due to some medical problems he was having. I talked with Dr. French at the University Psychiatric Center, and he indicated that, based on what our information was, Adam did seem appropriate to be an inpatient, but they could not take him unless he was out of custody of the sheriff, at which time Adam was not. I went back and talked to Dr. McAfee and the doctor felt that, due to Adam's problem and his age, that he might be better placed at the Adult Unit at LaRue Carter. He said if I made a referral to the Adult Unit, to him, he would walk the papers through for me for placement. We received information from Mr. Nellie and from a medical doctor in Indianapolis who had performed some testing in the past on Adam. Dr. McAfee referred it to the Adult Unit. They contacted me and said he was not an appropriate candidate based on his being an inmate at the Miami County Jail. I did not seek any other…"

"Because what?"

"He was an inmate at the Miami County Jail. They had no security measures whatsoever at that point. They also said that they needed a medical referral. So, when bond was set for Adam, and we set aside the custodial problem, Mr. and Mrs. Mitchell had started with the psychiatric treatment and the medical examinations in Howard County, and that resulted in inpatient at St. Vincent's Stress Center at the time. I was not able to facilitate any inpatient program for Adam, due to his age and due to his being in custody of the sheriff."

"Are you generally familiar with psychiatric care facilities available in this state through the Juvenile Justice System?"

"No," Ms. Monaghan answered.

Judge Embrey said, "I think it's safe to say we haven't found any."

"No, my question is, is there any such thing then?" Mr. Grund asked.

"There is not. I believe that Logansport State Hospital has recently started an Adolescent Unit, but I felt that Adam's age at that time hindered sending him. He was just kind of borderline. I didn't feel that…most facilities will not take an adolescent into services after the age of seventeen, whether it be a private placement or a public."

"Do you feel that Adam's problems can be adequately treated within the Juvenile Justice System as it presently stands?"

"No, I do not."

"No further questions." Mr. Grund took his place back at the Prosecutor's table.

Mr. Fleming gently pushed his chair back and started taking his turn at the witness.

"Ms. Monaghan, you have received various reports from doctors, have you not, in the course of your investigation during the past few weeks?"

"Yes."

"Would you just outline and list to the Judge what you have in your file? What doctors have made reports?"

"A Dr. Bao, who is a medical doctor in Kokomo, performed quite a few tests, medical testing, on Adam. It appeared to be an EEG, which was within normal range, auditory evoked response, um, visual evoked response test. Um, and they found him to be medically okay."

"Let's have those marked for the record. There are five pages I'll mark as one exhibit."

"I handed you Exhibit A. Is this the exhibit that contains the report you just talked about?"

"Yes, it is."

"No objection," Mr. Grund said.

The Judge briefly looked at the documents. "Let's show Defense Exhibit A, in five parts, introduced without objection."

"You also have a report there from the Kennedy Clinic?" Mr. Fleming asked the witness.

"Yes, I do."

"I'll hand you what has been marked as Defendant's Exhibit B. Is this the Kennedy Clinic report?"

"Yes, it is."

"Offer that, Judge." Mr. Fleming handed the Judge another document.

"No objection."

"We'll show Defense Exhibit B introduced without objection," the Judge said.

"Do you have any other reports, Ms. Monaghan?"

"No, I do not."

"So, you are aware, in this particular case, that before our hearing today, we had a conference and we have a tentative agreement, which is commonly referred to as a plea bargain?"

"Yes."

"In the event that the Judge would not accept that plea bargain, are you still of the same opinion about transferring this case to Adult Court?"

"Yes, I am."

"And that is mainly because there is very little in the way of opportunities for Adam in the Juvenile Justice System?"

"That's correct."

"That's all, Judge."

"Anything further?" the Judge asked.

"Nothing further, your Honor," answered the prosecutor.

"You may step down. Any other witnesses, Mr. Grund?" the Judge asked.

"No, we have no further evidence to introduce, your Honor," answered Mr. Grund.

"Mr. Fleming?"

"No, Judge. I think for our record, though, I will state that as you are aware we have made negotiations before hearing and this hearing is a formality, I think, of our agreement in this case to waive Adam to Adult Court."

"You have, in effect, agreed to waiver?"

Adam answered, "Yes, sir."

"I still think it's incumbent upon the Court to make findings which would substantiate your waiver, and the Court will make the following findings: That Prosecuting Attorney has moved to have the juvenile charges transferred to Adult Court, where the Respondent there would stand trial as an adult; that the most serious charges filed against the Respondent Child is Reckless Homicide, Indiana code 35-42-1-5; that the Court finds there is a probable cause to believe the Respondent committed the act alleged; that the Respondent was 17 years of age at the time the alleged act was committed; that the Respondent is now 18 years of age; that the Probation Department of Miami County, or the Miami County Probation Department, has made an effort to find a psychiatric facility that could treat the Respondent as a juvenile and has found none; that there has been no showing that the best interest of the child or that the safety and welfare of the community would be better served by leaving the Respondent within the Juvenile System; and, therefore, the Court will order the Respondent Adam A. Mitchell waived to Adult Court. The Prosecutor has pre-filed the charges and the Adult Cause will be F-33-82S. Do you have a copy of the information, Mr. Fleming?"

"I'll get that, Judge."

"And that will conclude the juvenile matter. Are we now ready to proceed with the arraignment in the adult matter, or would you like to talk with your client for a few minutes first?"

"Uh, let's straighten the records out. Are Count 2 and Count 3 part of this? I don't think they are."

"Well, they were all three waived? I'm not sure what our records say," Mr. Grund added.

The Judge spoke, "They are all three waived."

"Your Honor, the matter is really academic in any case. What I was going to ask the Court to do is simply to arraign on the reckless homicide and not even arraign on the other two charges," Grund said.

"I agree, it is academic, but I don't think you actually waived the other two charges," said Fleming.

"I don't think, under this, I can't waive them under that same provision of the statute, and I don't think we can meet the waiver criteria under any other section of the statute. There's a different showing required. I think the best thing for us to do is show reckless homicide waived and ignore the other two charges, if you will, and arraign only on reckless homicide, that being Count 1 of the information. Mr. Mitchell, if you'll look at the document, I'll have Mr. Fleming point out to you where Count 1 is, and we'll read through that together. It reads: 'State of Indiana versus Adam A. Mitchell, information for Reckless Homicide. Kenneth F. Roland, being first duly sworn upon his oath, says that on or about the 6th day of July 1982, in the County of Miami and State of Indiana, one Adam A. Mitchell did recklessly kill Robert J. Lather, by operating his vehicle at a high rate of speed and striking the rear of the vehicle driven by Robert J. Lather, all of which is contrary to the form of the statute, in such cases made and provided to-wit, Indiana Code section 35-422-1-5, and against the peace and dignity of the State of Indiana.' This charge, as it is filed, is a Class C Felony. Mr. Mitchell, do you have any questions about the charges?"

"No, sir."

"Okay. Do you understand that a Class C Felony carries a standard sentence of five years of imprisonment, to which three years may be added for aggravating circumstances, or three years subtracted for mitigating circumstances, and a fine of up to $10,000?"

"Yes, sir."

"Do you understand that all or part of that sentence could be suspended?

"Yes, sir."

"Okay. Are we ready to proceed, then, with the remainder of the arraignment? Do you understand that you have the right to a trial in this charge, now as an adult, Mr. Mitchell?

"Yes, sir."

"Do you understand that you are presumed innocent, and that at a trial the State of Indiana would have to prove your guilt beyond a reasonable doubt with no requirement on your part to prove anything?

"Yes, sir."

The Judge continued asking Adam, do you understand this, do you understand that? I knew that Adam didn't understand all of the questions the Judge was asking him. But, Adam continued saying, "Yes, Sir," to everything that the Judge asked him.

"Do you have any questions about those rights?"

"No, sir."

"Do you understand at this point in time the Court will ask you to enter a plea? How do you...do you intend to have him enter his guilty plea today?"

"Yes, Judge, pursuant to our arrangement," Mr. Fleming said.

"All right, and the, I think the best thing to say is that the plea would be pursuant to a written agreement to be filed."

"Yes, and I can state for the record what our agreement is, and I'd like to do that." Fleming said.

"All right."

"Our agreement with the State is that in return for a plea of guilty to this charge, Mr. Mitchell will receive a five year sentence; that that sentence will be suspended; that he will be placed on probation with the Miami County Probation Department for a period of five years. As a condition of probation, will be the regular terms of probation, also that he will participate in inpatient or other such treatment program, as the Court or Probation Department may deem appropriate, and any change in his circumstances regarding treatment are subject to Court approval. He will receive good time credit for that time spent in the Miami County jail, as well as time for out-of-home inpatient or institutional placement. He will surrender his driving privileges and not apply to drive an automobile during the term of his probation. The State will not pursue the charges of Causing Death While intoxicated and Fleeing a Police Officer."

"Mr. Grund, is that substantially the agreement as you understand it to be?" Judge Embrey asked.

"Substantially so, your Honor. I would state to the Court that essentially, this plea has not been as a result of any agreement, it's been the result of Mr. Fleming contacting me, indicating their intentions that there was not factually much at issue in this case, with which we agree, and I would state to the Court that essentially this recommendation on the part of the Prosecutor's Office would have been the same regardless of whether or not there had been a trial in this matter." Mr. Grund paused before continuing.

"I have discussed it with the family of the victim, the State Police, and I think we are all in agreement that there is no good purpose to be served by incarcerating Mr. Mitchell with the Department of Corrections, but that it is everyone's desire that he receive all such inpatient treatment as is necessary in a psychiatric care facility to see that there is no more danger to society as a result of him being released from a program. We would further believe that since his entire treatment for this five-year period would be subject to the Court's approval. It would be our understanding that if that approval would be with prior notice to the Prosecutor's Office if there would be any changes in the nature of his treatment program."

Judge Embrey stated, "I might make an observation, and that is that the sentence as it's agreed to between the two of you seems to be a no confidence vote for the Department of Corrections for dealing with these problems, is that essentially correct? He could very easily spend five years in an inpatient program under this probation, which would be two-and-a-half years longer than he would spend in prison."

"Well, not if the Court is giving good time credit for all days," Fleming added.

"All right, as a term of probation he continues to get psychiatric treatment. If, in fact, he were sent to, for example, LaRue Carter, and at the end of two-and-a -half years, if he needed further treatment, under the terms of this plea agreement, he would remain institutionalized, possibly through the entire five-year period. Is that…?"

"I would agree," said Fleming.

"Okay, so the potential for restriction on his freedom could be greater under this agreement than if he were simply imprisoned under a five year sentence, in which case he would get good time credit for jail time, and would serve the balance of two-and-a-half years as long as he behaves well. My first reaction was that if the Department of Correction were, in fact, providing any kind of psychiatric treatment, which it is supposed to, probably the sentence could be sent to the Department of Corrections with a recommendation of psychiatric care. Our experience has been that you can recommend all you want, but you don't get, in the Department of Corrections, psychiatric treatment. Is that a fair assessment, do you believe?" the Judge added.

"Well, it is, but from my experience in dealing with the doctors in this case, it is not our position, nor that of the doctors who have seen Adam, that he is mentally ill. That is not our position. So, I would agree with you that the Department of Corrections would not treat him in that fashion as a mentally ill inmate. Therefore, I agree, he would not get any special treatment with the Department of Corrections."

"Okay. Mr. Mitchell, do you understand the terms of the plea agreement as explained to you by counsel?"

"Yes, sir."

"Do you understand that this has to be a reduced to writing and presented to the Court, and that your counsel and Mr. Grund are in the process of doing that?"

"Yes, sir."

"Do you understand that if you enter a plea of guilty, as it has been represented to me that you will, you give up the rights I explained to you just a few minutes ago?"

"Yes, sir."

"Do you understand that you're giving up the right to a trial, and you understand that you're giving up the presumption of innocence and the State does not have to prove your guilt?"

"Yes, sir."

"And do you understand that you will not get to see witnesses called against you, or call witnesses in your own behalf, regardless of the proof of your guilt or lack of guilt?"

"Yes, sir"

"Do you understand that you're giving up the right to an appeal by pleading guilty?"

"Yes, sir."

"I'm supposed to say that. The fact is everyone gives up the right to an appeal, I don't know why, but that's a part of the explanation. Do you have any questions at all about the rights you give up by pleading guilty?"

"No, sir."

"Do you understand that a plea of guilty means you're telling me you're guilty of all the elements of the crime against you. That is, that you did kill Robert J. Lather by reckless operating of your vehicle at a very high rate of speed, striking the rear of the vehicle driven by Robert J. Lather?"

"Yes, sir."

"Do you have any reservations about that admission whatsoever?"

"No, sir."

"All right, then I'll ask you for the record, to the charge of Reckless Homicide, how do you plea, guilty or not guilty?

"Guilty."

"And this is done pursuant to a plea agreement that is to be later filed?"

"Yes, sir."

"Has anyone promised you anything, other than this plea agreement?

78

"No, sir."

"Do you understand the Court was not a party to the agreement? The Court will have to, at one point, at some point in time, decide whether or not to accept the agreement."

"Yes, sir."

"Do you understand that if the Court accepts the agreement, it is bound by the sentence recommended by the Prosecuting attorney?"

"Yes, sir."

"Has anyone threatened you in any way, to cause you to enter the plea of guilty?"

"No, sir."

"Do you understand this charge completely?"

"Yes, sir."

"And the possible penalty?"

"Yes, sir."

"Do you understand that if you violate the terms set for you by the Court that you could still wind up serving the five year sentence?"

"Yes, sir."

"And that if you do violate the terms set for you by the Court that the deal is off, the terms of psychiatric treatment in lieu of imprisonment, and that you would, in fact, go to prison?"

"Yes, sir."

"Are you entering your plea freely and voluntarily?"

"Yes, sir."

"Do you believe Mr. Fleming has represented you fairly in this matter?"

"Yes, sir."

"I will tentatively accept the plea agreement, subject to the filing of the plea agreement and subject to acceptance of the terms of the plea agreement, after seeing the Pre-Sentence Investigation."

"Your Honor, one other question that possibly the Court asked, I do not recall it. Since he is in an inpatient care facility at the present time, I'm not sure if the Court asked if he was presently receiving any prescription medications at this time?" Mr. Grund asked.

"Yes, sir."

"And how recently did you take that medication?"

"I'm not sure when the last time…the last time that I can recall was last night"

"Last night?"

"About 10:30."

"What kind of medication is that?"

"It's Adapin."

"And what affect does that have on you?"

"It attacks your central nervous system."

"And does what?"

"Just…I'm not sure exactly what it does."

"Does it interfere with your ability to comprehend and understand what's going on around you?"

"No, sir."

"And, more to the point, do you believe that that medication has interfered in any way with your ability to understand and comprehend this charge and the possible penalty?"

"No, sir."

"And has it had any influence on your decision to enter a plea of guilty?"

"No, sir."

"I think that will take care of it."

"I believe so," said Mr. Grund.

"All right, then as soon as the plea agreement is filed, the Court will order that the Probation Office prepare a Pre-Sentence Investigation, and will set the matter for a Sentencing Hearing and present the evidence, proof of the Corpus Delicit, and so forth, at that time."

"Your Honor, could we possibly set the Sentencing Hearing at this time?" Mr. Grund asked.

Mr. Fleming stood. "Judge, we would like to get back, the reason I say get back in as soon as possible, this…the doctors feel that having this over Adam's head has been one of his emotional problems, so we'd like to get back in as soon as possible."

"Understood."

"With all that Ms. Monaghan has done, it may not take very long to put together a Pre-Sentencing report," Fleming said.

The Clerk of the court said, "Monday November 1 at 1:00. We can squeeze it in before the regular 1:00."

"Okay. Let me indicate, there are a couple of things that I want Miss Monaghan to look at, because I think there are factors that, while my inclination is to go along with the plea agreement of the victims, and if we're considering the parents and the wife of Officer Lather to be the victims, if the victims find it agreeable, I think there are some unknowns that we need to nail down a little bit. While we have said that changes in treatment are subject to Court approval, we all know as a practical matter, the Court cannot order the Department of Mental Health to do something it doesn't want to do. It never works. I'd like to know what the prognosis is. Are we talking about…when are we talking about their prediction for him to be released. Is it to be…are they going to recommend a gradual kind of a thing? How long do they anticipate him being an inpatient? If things go well, what are the parameters on that…the shortest period and the longest period that they could foresee? What kind of outpatient treatment do they anticipate? Do they anticipate a halfway house? I'd like to know what their program is, and, you know, if they tell me he's going to be here one more month then we're going to discharge him, that's going to be a whole lot of difference than six months inpatient, six months in half-way house, three years in out-patient treatment. I don't know what we're talking about in terms of treatment at this point. I find this crime, while it is not a crime that requires specific intent, one where I'm not willing to make a public statement that you just get thirty to sixty days worth if psychiatric treatment and that's all you need."

"Your Honor, that's the reason that we struck the plea agreement the way we did, that we're not leaving it up to doctors to determine when he is to be released or not released. We're leaving it up to the Court. They are going to have to apply to the Court before they can change his treatment."

"They're not part of this agreement, though. I can affect things that are optional and make his decision for him, but I can't change the doctors' conclusion that he is now to be released. Is the Department of Mental Health going to go along with this?"

"Effectively not. He's not under the control of the Department of Mental Health. The Department of the State and the Department of Mental Health can do whatever they want to do," Mr. Grund said.

"All right."

"He's at a private facility," Fleming added.

"He's at a private facility, but will they keep him on a Court order to do so? Will they keep him there as long as the Court says keep him there?"

"Yes, sir, I think if they were adamant that he no longer needed hospitalization, they probably wouldn't keep him. It is our intention with this, that at such time that he no longer needs hospitalization, that there is some sort of a half-way house, work release program, whatever you want to call it, which is going to take some finding in terms of Diana's looking for it, and so forth. Which, I am sure, one of those programs would accept him. I don't think there's any..." Mr. Grund said.

"That's what I wanted to know. Are all those things practical? Are we actually going to be able to do what we set out to do with this plea agreement? Because I think a substantial restriction on liberty is a natural consequence of this kind of act, and if it can be restricted in a psychiatric facility where he can really have some help, that's fine with me. But I don't want to find out in thirty days the doctors are going to say, that's all he needs and send him back home. I will not go along with that, so I need to know what we're talking about."

"That was our expectation, that the Court wouldn't go along with something like that, and that's the reason we did the plea agreement in the manner we did," answered Mr. Grund.

"Well, we want the Court to think that if the professionals felt that Adam is ready for a half-way environment, and then to be released back into society, that the Court would stand in the way of that. If the doctors and professional people who were treating Adam felt that way, just because of the type of case this is involving a police officer..." Mr. Fleming said.

"The fact this involves a police officer, I don't think, is the only element the Court needs to look at. We have an out of control seventeen year old, screaming down the highway at more than ninety miles an hour, killing somebody. There's a consequence for that," said the Judge.

"He was being treated by *'professionals'* at that point in time. That's why I think that this Court is probably in a much better position than some of the quote *professionals* to determine when persons need treatment and when they don't," Mr. Grund said.

"And I think one of the reasons the Court is willing to go along with this is not just because of the psychiatric treatment, but because there appears to be a very substantial restraint of liberty. At the age Adam is, at eighteen, if we sent him to the Department of Corrections, we'd be dealing with him probably the rest of his life. The Department of Corrections will not help him, but will hurt him. It has no interest in doing anything for him psychologically. And I think, probably, that he does need psychiatric help. But I'm looking at this time, at a psychiatric facility, not just from the standpoint of psychiatric treatment, but as a restraint of liberty, I think. He's got that coming after this act that was committed. There has to be punishment involved, in some fashion and substantial punishment when a life is taken and done in such a reckless manner. And I'm just not going to go along with the psychiatrist saying thirty days from now, 'Okay his head's all right, he can go back, back on the street.' I just, I don't see that as reasonable. So, again, my reason for accepting the plea agreement is because I perceive it as involving very substantial restrictions on his liberty. Okay, we will be back then in the first, is that the date, for sentencing. The Pre-Sentence will be finished at that time, hopefully some of these questions will be answered."

"That's at one o'clock on the first?" Mr. Grund asked.

"Huh?" said the Judge.

"One o'clock on the first?"

"Yes. Mrs. Mitchell thank you for being so cooperative with everyone in this matter. Miss Monaghan has mentioned to me, and so has Mr. Grund, that you've been very, very, cooperative in dealing with the issues we're dealing with. It makes it a lot easier. Anything further?"

"About the only other thing, your Honor, occurs to me is he simple remains released…" said Grund.

"On the same terms?" asked the Judge.

"On the same terms that he is to be returned to the inpatient care facility at St. Vincent's."

"As I recall, at the time the Court…"

"There has really been no order in the criminal action, I guess, is what I'm saying," said Grund.

"There has not."

"So, probably there should be an order of some nature in the criminal action."

"But one of the orders issued in the Juvenile action, I believe, spoke to that issue. No. The court will order, in the adult matter, that the…I will transfer the order of August 24th, 1982, to the Adult case and will deem him to be released under that same order, with the $3,000 cash bond having been posted, being the bond in this case. Is that agreeable? Transfer the bond from the Juvenile matter to the Adult matter, with the same restrictions?"

"Yes, except technically, under the Juvenile order, he could have been released back to his parents, it would not be my expectation that he would be released from inpatient facility that he has been in presently, without further order of the Court," Grund continued.

"I think our agreement at the time that I entered this order, and it didn't find its way into the order, was that the terms would be the same for adult as juvenile release, and that the bond would carry over. We haven't had any problems, so far, with..."

"I have no problems with the bond carrying over. My problem is there's no restraint in terms of if he goes back to St. Vincent's today and tomorrow somebody decides to release him, that he'd be released without the Court knowing anything of it."

"Well, I'll order that the Court be notified immediately if there is to be any changes in his status, that is, an inpatient at St. Vincent's. Okay. Is there anything further?"

"No, your Honor."

# Chapter 8

After the trial I drove back to Kokomo so Adam could spend some time at home before he had to be back at the hospital in Indianapolis.

"Get extra clothes, so if I'm gone longer than a week, you'll have plenty until I get back," I called up the stairs to where Adam was in his bedroom. "We need to leave in just a few minutes. I'm almost packed."

Soon Adam came down the stairs. He had been crying. I took him in my arms and held him for a few minutes. "We'll get through this together, Adam. You know that if my mother wasn't so sick I wouldn't be leaving now."

"It's not that I don't want you to go to see Grandma. I was just thinking how long it will be before I can ever come back home and the fact that Dad didn't care enough about me to be with me today."

"Adam, I really don't think it's because your Dad doesn't love you that he wasn't there. I don't think he knows how to show love. He loves you or he wouldn't have bought you the car. I can't explain why other things seem more important to him than we do. But, Adam I love you enough for two people. Please, don't *ever* forget that." I hugged him again.

"Maybe after you get out of the hospital they'll have a halfway house lined up right away and you won't have to stay in jail that long. They're good to you there. Even the sheriff's wife said you don't belong in jail. You're not a criminal. You had an accident. There is a big difference between having an accident and deliberately doing something wrong. It would be wonderful if the government could afford to put the people who need punishment from accidents because of careless behavior in one facility and put the people who deliberately commit crimes in a separate place. You're a good person, Adam, and you have to remember that. I'll be there to see you, as often as they will let me. Between times I'll write to you as often as I can. In fact, if you want me to write to you every day I'll do that. I love you, Adam, and I always will. Now, let's get our things out to the car."

Neither one of us had much to say on the way back to St. Vincent's. I was afraid to say how I felt because I didn't want my son upset any more than he already was. I walked Adam back to the hospital ward and gave him a hug and kiss and told him I would see him in one week. I left him at the hospital, feeling I was sharing the sentence with my son. I couldn't be at ease with any of this until Adam had a grip on another life and was happy again.

I arrived at the airport, checked my luggage and immediately boarded the plane. I gave a sigh of relief that I had made it through one of the worst days of my life, and now it was up to the pilot to fly me to Savannah. I could have a few hours of rest while in the air.

I really didn't like to fly, but driving took too long and I just didn't feel up to making the trip by myself. I thought of Clay and wondered if he would at least call to see what the outcome of the trial was. I wondered how two people who had been so close could have grown so far apart.

I had been pregnant with Adam when I'd first met Clay. It was July the 4$^{th}$, 1964. My mother was visiting, to check on me and to see how I was doing. I had just met Carol and she was pregnant, too. We worked together and Carol had invited me to a picnic to celebrate Independence Day. At first I refused the invitation, but Carol had insisted, and when my mother came to Kokomo she had convinced me to get out and meet people. So, my mother and I had gone to the picnic. That was the first time I had met Clayton. Funny, it was the 4th of July that had brought us together and it looked like the 4th of July was the beginning of tearing us apart.

Carol introduced me to Clayton, but I was so distraught over being pregnant and not being married that I couldn't even remember his name. Later that evening when we were back at my apartment and recapturing the events of the day I asked, "Mama, what did Carol say that guy's name was? I can't remember."

"Clayton Mitchell. Seems like a good man to me."

Well, he didn't do anything for me, but back then I couldn't think about any man except Jack.

"He has a great smile and that one gold tooth added some character. His eyes are as blue as Paul Newman's."

I looked at my mother and smiled.

"He does have beautiful blue eyes and he's built like Hoss Cartwright."

We were laughing like a couple of school girls. My mother was not only my mother, she was my friend.

I looked at her olive skin, darken even more by the sun, her black hair and green eyes and her soft appearance. It was obvious that she had some Cherokee blood flowing in her veins. She had a sixth sense that was indescribable, and I remembered that she could cure warts. My mother possessed a sense of hospitality and kindness that was unmatched by any one I have ever met. It was good to have my mother with me. I would sleep well.

Several days later the phone rang.

"Hello."

"Hi, Paige. This is Clayton Mitchell. I was wondering if you would like to go for a pizza on Friday evening?"

"My mother is still here and…"

"I'm leaving early Thursday morning to drive back home," called Mama from the kitchen.

"I guess I could do that. My mother's leaving on Thursday morning. Yes, 6:00 will be fine. I'll be ready."

"Honey, I'm glad you're going to go out with him. He seems so kind and gentle. It'll do you good to get out, instead of sitting in the house all the time."

*Trinity Chapel United Methodist Church*

Mama left on Thursday and I started thinking about what I could find to wear to have dinner with Clayton Mitchell. I was getting larger and didn't have much of a selection of maternity clothes. I pulled out a pair of white pedal pushers and cut a half circle out of the front and attached a piece of bias tape to cover the raw edges and make a tie to hold them in place. After redoing a pair of pants, I had to find a top that would fit around my bulging middle. I found a pink and white variegated strip dress with a full skirt and made a maternity top out of the skirt part of the dress. No, it wasn't made from velvet curtains, like Scarlet had done, but it was a recreation. That was one thing my mother had taught me growing up, not to waste anything. I remember Mama making skirts out of Daddy's old pants.

I tried on my redone clothing. "I think I look rather attractive in my new pink and white outfit." My hair was as dark as my Mama's and my eyes a mix of my Daddy's brown eyes and a trace of my Mama's green eyes. The Cherokee bloodline was still obvious.

Clay was a few minutes early and was carrying a pink rose he had picked from a bush, and it probably wasn't his bush, I thought as he handed it to me.

"Hi. I brought you a flower."

"It's beautiful. Thank you. Let me put it in some water and I'll be ready." I put the pink rose in water and we left for what would be the first date I had had since Jack left.

Once in the car, Clay asked, "Have you ever had pizza from Rosie's Little Italy in Marion?"

"No, I haven't. I've been to Marion, but I've never been to Rosie's."

"They have fantastic pizza. I thought we would drive over there, if you didn't mind."

He seemed so trustworthy, and he was a friend of Carol's. I didn't feel afraid. "Sounds good to me."

We spent time telling each other about our lives and how we each had come to Kokomo. The longer I was around this man, the better I liked him.

The pizza was excellent and the evening was perfect.

Clayton asked, "Would you like to go to church with me on Sunday?"

"Yes." I was delighted that he had asked. But I felt I had to divulge the truth.

"Clay, you don't mind if I call you Clay, do you? Clayton seems so formal and Clay fits you better."

"You can call me anything you want."

"Well, I need to tell you something before we start making anymore dates. I'm pregnant and the baby's father is in the service. I'm not sure that you will want to date a pregnant girl."

"Carol told me you were pregnant. It doesn't make any difference to me. That happened before I met you, and I might add I think you're the most beautiful girl I have ever seen."

I smiled at him and wondered if God had sent this man to be a friend to me in my time of need.

We attended church on Sunday. It was a Baptist church. I hadn't thought to ask before what kind of a church he had planned to go to. I had been raised in a Baptist church on Tybee Island, Georgia, the "Chapel By The Sea." There was a peace there, being so close to the ocean. It gave me peace, too, just recalling the times I had attended there.

I remembered singing in the children's choir and one of my favorite hymns was "The Church in the Wildwood." I sat in the pew with Clay, wishing they would sing my favorite hymn. It was good being back in church. The service was interesting and I felt good about being with Clay. My first impression was quickly fading.

We continued to see each other for several weeks and Clay asked me to marry him before the baby was born. I knew he was completely different from Jack, and I knew in my heart that Clay would be a better husband and father. I wouldn't have to worry about him seeing other women. Clay was in love with me and I loved his strength, his gentle smile and, most of all, I loved how free I felt just being with him.

He made my birthday very special. He had bought me a maternity outfit. It was blue and pink with the colors divided diagonally with a wide strip of white material on the front of the top, and it had blue shorts. I could live with a man of his character forever.

We both went over to Carol's house and told her we were planning to be married.

"When's the wedding?"

"Well, Clay wants to be married before the baby is born, and I thought we should wait so he wouldn't be responsible financially for the child," I said.

"When is you baby due?" asked Carol.

"Sometime the middle of October."

Clay insisted we go ahead and get married. "Look at it this way: if I give the baby my name no one will ever know the difference. It will be better for the baby. I think my health insurance will cover the birth and that will be an expense that we won't have. Let's set a date."

Carol chimed in, "I think you should get married as soon as possible."

A date was set: August 21, 1964. I started thinking about what I would wear to be married in.

"We have another problem," I said.

"What's that?" asked Clay.

"Do they make maternity wedding dresses?"

Everyone laughed, and I joined in. They had thought I was being funny, but deep inside I had visions of a beautiful wedding one day, hopefully in a lovely garden on a warm and sunny day. Well, warm and sunny I could have, but the dress and garden would be just a dream. I started thinking in terms of sewing a high waisted dress that might camouflage being pregnant a little bit, but it would be hard to camouflage seven months of pregnancy.

I found a lightweight brocade fabric in a pale aqua and began sewing my wedding dress.

I called my friend Peggy. "Hi, Peg, you remember the fellow I told you about meeting on the fourth of July?"

"Yes, I do. In fact, I thought I should've met him before now," she answered.

"Well, you're going to meet him. He's asked me to marry him, and I said I would. I want you to be my bridesmaid. You were the first person I met when I moved to Kokomo. You've always been good to me. I feel like you know me better than anyone. Would you do that for me, Peggy?"

"Of course I will. I would be honored. When's the big day?"

"We're planning on August 21. I know that's not much notice. It's not going to be a big and glamorous wedding. When you're pregnant and someone loves you enough to want to marry you, that's enough. We're just having Carol and her husband Joe, Rosie and Jim and you and Lowell."

"Who are Rosie and Jim?" Peggy asked.

"They're friends of Clay's. They have *Rosie's Little Italy* in Marion. They have really good pizza. We'll have to go over there some evening. You'd like it. I've got lots to do. Thanks, Peggy, for agreeing to be my bridesmaid. I need to get busy sewing on my dress. I'll call you later with the exact details. Thanks again."

The minister at First Baptist Church wouldn't marry us under the circumstances until we agreed to a few sessions of counseling.

He thought of every reason possible for the two of us not to get married.

"What if the baby's father comes back and wants to marry you? How will you feel then?" he asked.

"I don't ever intend to see him again. I've written him a letter and told him I was going to be married and that he would never see this child. I'm not asking for any support for the baby. If for some reason this marriage between Clay and me doesn't work, I'll never ask Clay for support money for the baby either."

I was adamant. In my mind I felt like if Clay loved me enough to want to make a life for the three of us, the least I could do was be the very best wife possible. I wasn't sure my love for Clay was as strong as it should be, to be getting married, but he was a good man and I liked his big build, gentle smile, his love for life, and his eyes as blue as Paul Newman's. I had become accustomed to the gold tooth in front. He had a very gentle nature and a hairy chest and I felt secure in his arms.

Clay didn't tell me until after we were married that he gave his apartment up one day before the wedding and had to sleep in his car the night before we were married.

We had only been married four weeks when I called Pittsburgh Plate Glass Co. and asked to speak to Clay. "This is Mrs. Mitchell and I think I need to go to the hospital. Could you have my husband call me, please?" I hung up the phone and lay down with a towel between my legs. The blood wouldn't stop flowing.

There was a knock on the door, "Who is it?" I shouted.

"It's Lowell."

"Come on in, Lowell." He walked in the living room and could see immediately that I was in trouble. "Have you called Clay?"

"I just called him. The baby isn't due yet. The bleeding is getting worse. Could you get me another towel?"

Just then the door opened. Clay had a look of fear on his face as he entered the room. "Hon, what's going on?" In the time it took to start explaining the problem, Clay and Lowell carried me to the car and rushed me to the hospital.

The doctors explained that the placenta had broken loose and if I didn't start into labor soon they would have to induce it. It was a dangerous situation which might call for a c-section. The hours passed and the labor didn't come. The doctors induced labor and thirty hours later, Adam Allen Mitchell came into the world. Clay wanted to name him Adam Lee, because Clay's middle name was Lee, but I had to tell him that Jack's full name was Jack Lee Campbell. I didn't want Jack to think that I wanted Adam to have any part of his name. So, we agreed that Adam Allen would be better.

The nurse brought the baby to me. "He sure does look like his father," she said as she handed him to me. Clay and I just looked at one another and smiled. No one ever questioned him not being Clay's child.

"Would you like a drink?" the stewardess asked.

"A Coke would be fine, thanks."

It was dark outside, but clear, and I could see the bright lights below sparkling like diamonds. I sipped my Coke and wondered how I would break the news of Adam's accident to my mother.

Tybee Island had serenity to it that I was looking forward to experiencing. The past few months had been a living hell, and I was hoping to escape the anguish that I had been feeling by returning to Tybee. Growing up there was like no other place I had ever seen. The beach was my playground and if that wasn't enough I had the back river to fish in and the tidal creeks in which to scoop up fish with a crab net. My friend Sally and I had spent hours running on the beach learning to turn cartwheels, which I never perfected, and still couldn't do. We would roller-skate for hours at the skating rink that was built on the pavilion that extended out over the ocean. It was a good place to grow up and I loved coming home.

Only this time, I wouldn't find my mother standing at the kitchen sink as I had so many times before. I wondered if I would see any improvement since I had last seen Mama. It was heartbreaking for me to believe that my mother would never be the person she had been before.

Mama spent a lot of her time in the kitchen. She had Daddy put in a big window over the kitchen sink so she could see the Wisteria that was climbing and almost choking to death the large oak tree just outside.

I wondered if I would upset her by telling her the truth about why I hadn't come home to take care of her. I said a silent prayer as I heard the stewardess announce the time of our arrival in Savannah.

It was late when the plane landed and I found my youngest sister waiting for me at the airport.

"I'm so glad to see you, Tess." I gave my sister a hug.

"It's good to see you, too. How have you been? Everybody's been worried about you. How's Adam doing?"

"Wait a minute, one question at a time. I'm fine and I think Adam is in the best hands he could be in for the time being. It's going to be a long tough road, but we'll both survive. I want to thank you and Gordon for sending the money when I needed it for his attorney."

"You know I would do anything I could to help you, and you don't have to thank us. I remember another time you needed someone, and I wasn't there. I'll be there for you this time."

"If you're talking about when I was pregnant for Adam, we were both young then and I never felt like you weren't there for me. That's all in the past now. I have enough problems here and now. I don't need to dwell on what could have been. It's really good to be back in Savannah. Smell the Union Bag? You'd think when technology is so advanced that they can put a man on the moon, they could do something about that awful smell from the paper mills. Thank goodness that odor is mostly on the westside of town."

"Sometimes on the westside. It depends on the way the wind is blowing."

"Well, let's head to the beach. We won't smell it down there. How's Mama doing?"

"She seems to get a little better all the time. I'm surprised how Daddy has improved since Mama had her stroke. One day she was waiting on him hand and foot, and the next day he was by her side day after day in the hospital and trying to do all he could to help her."

"I'm sure they really love each other. They just didn't know how to show it in the right way."

Everyone was asleep when we arrived at our childhood home on Tybee Island. We fixed ourselves a glass of tea and sat on the porch talking quietly. You could hear the ocean lapping at the shore and feel the humidity in every breath. It was good to be home.

# Chapter 9

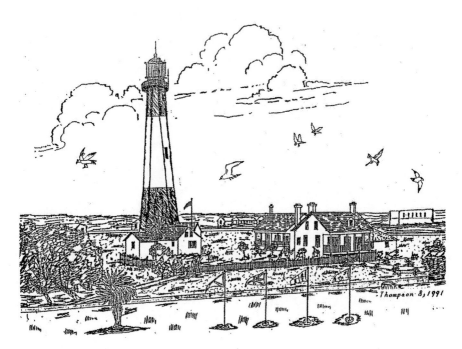

*Tybee Island Lighthouse - Georgia*

Everyone was up when I awoke to my sister Dorothy's voice. "Breakfast is ready!" I almost jumped from my bed. It was the best rest I had had for months, and I rushed to the kitchen to be with my parents.

Hugging my mother tightly and giving her a kiss I said, "It's really good to see you. I've wanted to come home for a long time to see how you were doing. Just look at you." I ran my hand over her head. "Your hair is growing out. It won't be long and you'll be wanting me to give you a permanent." I was surprised to see how well she looked.

She had her left arm in a sling and appeared to have gained some weight.

Still touching Mama I leaned over and gave Daddy a hug and kissed him on the head. "Looks like you are a pretty good nurse, Daddy." I winked at my older sister Dorothy.

"She gives me trouble sometimes," Daddy said.

Dorothy chimed in, "The other day we wanted to take her to town and she didn't want to go, said she's too much trouble with her wheelchair. Daddy told her it wouldn't be any trouble at all, he'd tie that wheelchair to the back bumper of the car, tie her hat on her head and we'd head to town."

Mama was laughing a little now. "You should see my wheelchair. When we're in a store, your Daddy has rigged up a flag that he puts on my chair so he can find me between the aisles."

"I lost her in K-Mart one day and I must have gone up and down every aisle in that store looking for her. That's when I got the idea. I just went over to the bicycle department and bought me one of those flags and tied it to her wheelchair, now I can keep up with her," he said proudly.

"At first when he would take me to the grocery store he'd push me so fast everything was just a blur, he would fly down those aisles and I couldn't see a thing. This way he can sit up front and watch the flag go up and down the aisles and we're both happier."

"Sounds to me like you have made some pretty good adjustments around here."

"How's Adam?" Mama asked. Everybody's eyes were watching to see how I would respond to her.

101

*Annette Bergman*

"What do you say we finish breakfast and I'll help you outside and we'll sit in the swing and I'll tell you about Adam, okay?"

We all ate a delicious southern breakfast of bacon, eggs, grits, biscuits and gravy. It was the best I had felt in months. I didn't know how to explain it, but there was nothing as satisfying as being at home on Tybee Island with my family. My inner child was happy.

After breakfast, I helped Mama outside and into the swing that was nestled beneath a huge old oak tree surrounded by Azalea bushes and a beautiful camellia bush that Mama had encircled with a row of bricks. Its branches were heavy with buds, and it amazed me that the Camellias always bloomed in December and January. The Spanish moss was hanging as graceful and diligently as ever. Just being home had made me almost forget about the stress I had been under. After getting Mama comfortable, the two of us starting gently swinging back and forth. I began telling mama the story and watching her expressions to be sure she wasn't getting upset. When I had finished I waited for her response. It was as if Mama couldn't comprehend the seriousness of Adam's situation.

"I knew there was a good reason that you hadn't come home to take care of me," she said at last.

I gave Mama a hug. "Mama, I wanted badly to be here for you, but I just couldn't leave Adam." The tears were streaming down my cheeks. "I hoped you understand. I just couldn't be in two places at once."

"It's okay. Your sisters have been very good to me and your daddy has done everything he could. You take care of Adam. I'm in good hands. How long will you be home?"

"I should be back in Indiana on Sunday so I can see Adam. I need to get back to work, and Clay will be coming home from Colorado on Sunday, too. I want to be there when he comes home. We have been having some problems since this accident and I'm hoping the time away from one another will do us some good. I'd like to take a walk on the beach while I'm here and just relax for a few days," I said. It was obvious that there was something missing in my mother. She wasn't emotional about Adam and I was reluctant to tell her any more than was necessary.

I spent hours walking on the beach and listening to the waves breaking on the shore. This had been my childhood playground and the sand felt good beneath my feet. I would walk in the edge of the surf pulling my feet through the water until my feet would get cold and then walk to the soft dry sand that had been warmed by the sun. The beach wasn't crowded in mid October and I sat on a fallen palmetto tree and wrote the troubles of my mind in the sand. Somehow writing my feeling in the sand and then erasing them had a healing effect and I sat for a long period of time writing positive and negative feelings that I had, mostly about my relationship with Clay. I knew I loved him deeply, but he wasn't as comforting and sympathetic as I needed him to be right now. In fact what I needed most was to feel loved and I didn't feel loved. Clay was good in a lot of ways, but showing affection wasn't one of his better traits. What I needed was to feel his strong arms around me and hear him say that he loved me, and that he would be there for Adam. I wasn't sure if he loved me or not and I understood how Adam felt.

It seemed that Clay loved his truck, and he loved his boat, and he loved to go deer hunting, and square dancing, and he loved to read *Field and Stream*. He would be sitting up late at night reading *Field and Stream* when I wanted him to go to bed with me. I had convinced myself that I was low on his list of priorities. This ate away at me like a cancer. I felt like the ice trays in the refrigerator. I kept them filled, but whenever I needed ice they were always empty. That's how I felt now: empty.

I thought I had done a good job keeping myself trim and looking good for Clay. I knew that I had been as good a wife as anyone could want. In fact, the men who worked with Clay was always commenting on the things I would do for Clay, like the lunches I packed for him. They told me he ate better than anyone in the Chrysler Plant. I had done things like putting notes in with his sandwiches or writing messages on his boiled eggs. I had even patched his jeans with red hearts sewn on them, and it had all been to no avail.

What Clay wanted was trucks, boats, campers, and to go square dancing and deer hunting. He couldn't be bothered by life's bumps in the road. He needed smooth sailing in calm waters.

I vowed before God, while watching a ship sail into the Savannah River, that Adam and I would come out of this better people. God didn't give people more than they can handle. Clay's mom was always saying that, and I believed it. She had given me a poem called "Love Conquers All." I wasn't sure if I believed that or not, for love was not at the heart of our marriage now.

I spent as much time as I could on the beach. It gave me rest and renewed my strength. I tried to give my sisters a break while I was there, and I wanted to be with my parents as much as possible. I didn't know when I would get back home and I wasn't sure about my mother's health either. I left for home early on Sunday morning.


It was around three in the afternoon when I arrived back at our home in Kokomo. I felt rested after my trip to Tybee. I had stopped by St. Vincent's Hospital to see Adam and he seemed to be coping with being institutionalized. I had made it home ahead of Clay. I put my things away, making several trips past the windows to see if Clay had pulled into the driveway yet. I had really missed him, or at least missed the man I had pictured in my mind. Sometimes I didn't think this was the same Clay I had married. The one I married was like a big fuzzy teddy bear, kind and gentle and seemed to love me with everything that was in him. We had been close in those early years and I had been so proud to be his wife. How could the love that we had shared become so hateful?

I heard the truck pull into the driveway. I ran to the kitchen and watched from the window. I felt my heart pounding and my mind saying *I really do love you, Clay.* He was coming in. I knew he would have to walk past me in the galley kitchen. I stood there waiting for him. I wanted to rush into his arms and tell him how much I had missed him. He looked at me with his clear blue eyes and said, "I started to turn around and come back several times. I missed you." I moved toward him and he pulled me to him. Looking down at me he said, "I missed my deer hunting and square dancing partner."

The telephone rang, I went to answer it and it was Brian from the office. "Glad to have you back. When did you get home?"

"Just about an hour ago," I answered.

"Is Clay back?" he asked.

"Yes, he just walked in the door."

"Then I'll let you go. I'll see you at the office first thing in the morning." Brian hung up.

"Who was that?" Clay said.

"It was Brian."

"It's always Brian. You talk to him more than you do to me," his soft demeanor had changed.

"Well, I suppose I do. You didn't miss me. You missed your deer hunting and square dancing partner. All you want me for is to go deer hunting and square dancing with. I'm more than a partner. I stood right here in this spot not too long after we moved into this house and asked you to make love to me one day and you said "I'm hungry, let's go get something to eat." I stated defiantly.

"I'll tell you one thing. I've taken all the rejection out of you I can handle. I've had plenty of offers and I've turned them all down. But I'll not turn down another one. You find yourself another deer hunting and square dancing partner. I'm done."

I hated myself for the way I had responded to Clay's attempt to work things out. The anger I felt was as much directed to the turmoil we had been through and Mama's ill health as it was to Clay. Clay just stood there with a puzzled look on his face.

I wondered how the conversation would have gone that day if Brian hadn't called at that exact moment. I started doing my normal thing, getting busy and hoping the problem would somehow solve itself. It was out of my control and I didn't know how to fix it.

106

Brian was a good friend and had been a big help to me at work, but his timing was awful.

I was going through the mail and found an Editorial that someone sent to me from the *Peru Tribune* that read:

### Punishment Needed

Yesterday's paper reported the plea bargain in the case of Adam Mitchell, the Kokomo youngster responsible for the death in July of Indiana State Trooper Robert Lather, Jr.

Fleeing Howard County police, the intoxicated, 17-year-old Mitchell rammed the rear of Lather's patrol car as Lather was trying to head him off.

The plea bargain had Mitchell plead guilty to reckless homicide, and, if Judge Bruce Embrey accepts the bargain at sentencing Nov.1, he would be given a five-year suspended sentence. During his five years of probation, he would lose his driver's license and the court would supervise some combination of in-patient and out-patient treatment for the somewhat emotionally disturbed Mitchell.

In agreeing to the plea bargain, Prosecutor James H. Grund was, we presume, acting with commendably humane motives in trying to see that Mitchell gets help and that the tragic crime of July 5 not be repeated.

We feel, however, that the agreement is unbalanced, for surely such an outrageous crime as Mitchell's demands some punishment, too.

Mixing punishment in Indiana with effective counseling and therapy is very difficult, given the resources of the State Department of Corrections. But we feel a mixture might have been found and should have been pursued.

This plea bargain leaves a sour taste in the mouth, and we urge Judge Embrey to reject it. That way the case would go on the trial calendar, perhaps to be the subject of a new, better plea bargain.

How can a Plea Bargain be published in the newspaper? Isn't this case to be decided in the courtroom? I wonder if this case involved the son of the article writer, if he would feel the same way?

# Chapter 10

Adam had to go back to court on November the first for his sentencing. I was allowed to pick him up and drive him to the Miami County Courthouse.

I was pleased that Adam seemed to be getting better since he had been in the hospital, but still he had a medicated look about him.

I gave him a hug when I arrived at the hospital. Adam had been standing close to the door waiting for me. "Well, today's the big day. Are you ready?"

"I'll feel better when it's over. I've made up my mind that I can do it."

I dreaded the trip back to the courtroom, but we had no choice and Adam was right. The sooner we got this over with the better off we would be.

"Be it remembered on the 1st day of November, 1982, the same being Calendar Year 1982, the above and foregoing cause of action came to be heard before the Honorable Bruce C. Embrey, sole Judge of the Miami Superior Court." The Bailiff had his job to do. It certainly wasn't a job I would want, seeing people in trouble with the law day in and day out.

"This is Cause Number F-33-82S, State of Indiana verses Adam A. Mitchell. Mr. Fleming, you represent Mr. Mitchell. The State of Indiana is represented by James H. Grund, Prosecuting Attorney. At a hearing on October 12, 1982, the Court was presented with an oral plea agreement. The Court questioned the defendant, I believe, as to rights he was giving up. Is that correct?"

"Yes, I think we went through that," Mr. Fleming said.

"We went through that. I am going to go back through the plea agreement with him, however, now that we have it in writing. The Court accepted the plea, reserving the right to reject it after seeing the pre-sentence investigation and hearing any testimony that was presented. Mr. Mitchell. Is that plea agreement in front of you at this time?"

"Yes."

"And is it your signature that appears on the second page of the plea agreement? And did you read that agreement in its entirety?"

"Yes, Sir."

"Do you understand that the charges to which you entered your guilty plea on October 12th is reckless homicide, a Class C felony?"

"Yes."

"Specifically, that on the 6th day of July 1982, in Miami County, Indiana, you did recklessly kill Robert J. Lather by operating your motor vehicle at a high rate of speed, striking the rear of the vehicle driven by Robert J. Lather, contrary to Indiana law."

"Yes, Sir."

"Okay. Do you understand that the prescribed sentence for a Class C felony is a fixed term of imprisonment for five years with not more than three years subtracted for mitigating circumstances, and in addition, a fine of not more than $10,000?"

"Yes, Sir."

"Do you understand that all or part of that sentence could be suspended, as well as the fine?"

"Yes, Sir."

"Do you understand that the agreement that has been entered between your attorneys is that the Driving While Intoxicated and Resisting Law Enforcement would be dismissed, that you would be given a five year sentence to the Department of Corrections?  That sentence would be suspended on the condition that you: 1. participate in inpatient or other such treatment programs as the Court or the Probation Department deem necessary or appropriate, and any change in the nature of the treatment is subject to the Court's approval; 2. that you receive credit for good time, for out-of-home inpatient or institutional placement; 3. that you not drive or operate a motor vehicle, and that you not reapply for a driver's license during the five-year period of probation; and 4. that you abide by the regular rules of probation?"

"Yes, Sir."

"Do you understand, as well, that on page two of the agreement, you're giving up a number of legal rights?"

"Yes, Sir."

The Judge continued with his do you understand this and do you understand that, things he had covered on the previous court hearing.

"Do you understand that you are giving up the right to the assistance of counsel at trial and at appeal, should you be convicted at a trial?"

"Yes."

"Do you understand that you are giving up the right to have counsel appointed for you for trial and appeal should you not be able to afford counsel?"

"Yes, Sir."

"All right, do you understand the Court is still not a party to this plea agreement?"

"Yes, Sir."

"I've had some discussions outside the courtroom with the prosecuting attorney and with your council, Mr. Mitchell, regarding the intent of the agreement and the extent to which the Court has the right to alter the treatment or punishment that is given under the terms of the agreement. I believe Mr. Fleming has discussed that with you. Is that correct?"

"Yes, Sir."

"And, has he told you, and do you understand the agreement to mean that if the Court determined your incarceration was appropriate, that the Court could order your incarceration during the period of the probation?"

"Yes."

"Do you understand that the Court could determine, at some time, to stop treatment and order you to be placed at the Department of Corrections or the Miami County Jail for the balance of the five years?"

"Yes, Sir."

"But do you understand there is a possibility that you could serve all or part of this sentence in either the Department of Corrections or the Miami County Jail?"

"Yes, Sir."

"Mr. Fleming, is that your understanding?"

"Well, as I understand it, the Department of Corrections is an option that might take mutual agreement, otherwise we're talking about the Miami County facility."

"All right. Mr. Grund?"

"That would be my understanding also, except under circumstances where probation was violated."

"All right. We've also had some discussion, Mr. Mitchell, that you should be aware of. I think Mr. Fleming has communicated this to you, but I think we need to place this on record. Upon your release from St. Vincent's Stress Center, the Court will order that you only be released to the Miami County Sheriff, that you then be transported to the Department of Corrections for a reception-diagnostic study and that after that study is completed, Mr. Fleming has the right to ask the Court to simple sentence you to the Department of Corrections."

"Yes, Sir."

"All right. Now, so that the record is very clear on this, those terms are not expressed very precisely in the agreement, but it is my understanding that counsel have agreed that those terms are within the Court's powers under this plea agreement. Is that correct, Mr. Grund, the modification sentence?"

"Yes, your Honor."

"Mr. Fleming, is that your understanding?"

"Yes, Sir."

"All right. I had expressed some reservations concerning the agreement at the hearing at which we took the guilty plea. Our discussions have clarified the powers that the Court has. The Court is being substituted, in effect, for the Department of Corrections in decision making as to where Mr. Mitchell is placed. Mr. Fleming, other than this agreement, have there been any promises made to you?"

"No, Sir."

"Mr. Mitchell, other than this agreement, have there been any promises made to you concerning this offense or this sentence?"

"No, Sir."

"Are you under the influence of alcohol or drugs or controlled substance of any kind at this time?"

"Yes."

"And is this medication from the Stress Center?"

"Yes, Sir."

"And what medications are those?"

"Uh, Senaquan and Compazine, Milantin, and I think that's it."

"Do those medications interfere in any way with your ability to understand the charges or the possible penalty or the terms of this agreement?"

"No, Sir."

"How recently have you taken the medication?"

"About an hour before I came."

"Is there any reason at all why you cannot, at this time, understand the charges to which you are entering a plea of guilty and also, the penalty that would be imposed if the court accepts that agreement?"

"No, Sir."

"Then do you believe it's in your best interest that the Court accept your plea of guilty?"

"Yes, Sir."

"Are you doing so…are you entering your plea freely and voluntarily?"

"Yes, Sir."

"Do you believe Mr. Fleming has represented you fairly in this matter?

"Yes, Sir."

"I think the Court has previously tentatively accepted the plea of guilty. Mr. Grund, I don't believe you presented any proof of Corpus Delicti. Do you wish to do that at his time?"

"Yes, your Honor. Call Kenneth Roland."

"Be seated. You testified at the waiver hearing at the time of the entry of the plea?"

"Yes, Sir."

"Detective Roland, did you investigate the death of Robert J. Lather?"

"Yes, Sir, I did."

"I'll show you what's been filed with the Court as a pre-sentence investigation of Adam Mitchell. Attached to that is a case report of several pages. I'll ask you whose signature is on that report?"

"That's my signature."

"And are the contents of that report true and correct at the time that the report was made, as well as presently?"

"Yes, Sir."

"Your Honor, I'd move the Court to accept the case report of Detective Roland which is included as part of the pre-sentence investigation as Corpus Delicti"

"Any objection, Mr. Fleming?"

"We'd stipulate to that, Judge."

"Stipulated into evidence as proof of Corpus Delicti. Do you have any further questions for Officer Roland?"

"No further evidence, your Honor."

"Mr. Fleming, any cross-examination?"

"No, Sir."

"You may step down. Anything further to add to the Corpus Delicti, Mr. Grund?"

"No, your Honor"

"Mr. Mitchell, is there anything you'd like to say concerning the offense itself?"

"No, Sir."

"And are you in agreement that the report by the Indiana State Police is accurate?"

"To the best of my knowledge, yes."

"You have also given a statement to the Probation Department, have you not, concerning your version of the offense?"

"Yes Sir, I did."

"Is there anything you wish to change in your version of the offense at his time?"

"No, Sir."

"I'll note for the record, the Court will also consider the defendant's version of the offense in proof of the Corpus Delecti. Mr. Grund, do you wish to be heard further before the Court enters a tentative finding at least?"

It seemed like the Judge was being mighty careful about noting for the record.

"No, your Honor, not with regard to the finding of guilty."

"Mr. Fleming?"

"No, Judge."

"All right. I have tentatively accepted the plea of guilty. I will tentatively enter a finding of guilty, and at the conclusion of the pre-sentence hearing will determine once and for all whether to accept the terms of the agreement. Have you reviewed the pre-sentence investigation with Mr. Mitchell and his family?"

"Yes, Judge."

"Are there any additions or corrections that need to be made?"

"No, Sir."

"Mr. Grund, do you wish to present any evidence."

"We call Bob Bryan."

A rather heavy man with brown hair that looked as though it hadn't been washed for several days stood. His shirt was unevenly tucked in and his trousers looked like he had weighed twenty pounds more at one time. He walked to the witness box and took his seat facing us. Now I noticed his eyes were wide, like he didn't know what was in store for him.

"Would you state your name and occupation, please?"

"Bob Bryan, reporter for the Peru Daily Tribune."

"And Bob, in the course of your duties for the Peru Daily Tribune, do you report almost all of the Court news?"

"Yes, I do."

"And you were present in the court at the time that the waiver hearing took place on this case. Is that correct?"

"Yes, I was."

"And you reported that in the Peru Daily Tribune?"

"Yes, I did."

"Following that report in there, there was an editorial that appeared in the Tribune with regard to the plea agreement that was proposed in that matter. Are you familiar with that editorial?"

"Yes, I am."

"Okay, was that editorial prepared with your assistance?"

"I wrote it."

"So then essentially, I take it, it reflects your views and the views of the local newspaper?"

"I advised my bosses that I was writing such an editorial and if they agreed with it, I would like them to publish it. That's what happened."

"Okay, now the editorial expresses, in fact urges, the judge to reject this agreement that has been entered into the record today. Is that correct?"

"Yes, it does."

117

"I take it at this time, you still disagree with this proposed handling of this case."

"That would depend upon the understandings that have been reached today. If the understandings are that the Judge has the power to punish, as well as help this young man, then I would have no quarrel with it."

"Were you present in court at the time that the agreement was orally presented to the Judge?"

"Yes, I was."

"Do you recall the Judge, at that time, indicating that he would feel free and felt that punishment of some nature could be indicated in this case also?"

"Yes, I do."

"So what you are saying is, so long as that remains an open option, you on behalf of the newspaper at least, feel that this would be an appropriate disposition of the case?"

"I would think it ought to be more than simply an option. I think it ought to be in the plans in this case, but I wouldn't quarrel as long as the Judge has the option of imposing some punishment somewhere down the line."

"But you would feel comfortable with leaving it up to the Judge's discretion, whether it be treatment, punishment or whatever?"

"Yes, I would feel more comfortable if he would announce that there was some punishment pending in this case, but I certainly would not quarrel with if…leaving it as you put it, leaving it as his option."

"Do you believe in enforcing the laws in the state of Indiana?"

"I don't enforce them. I mean are you talking about…"

"No, I said do you believe in enforcing them? Do you agree that the laws of the state should be enforced?"

"Yes, I do."

"Okay, are you familiar with the Constitution of the State of Indiana?"

"The part about punishment not being…that rehabilitation is the object of the law?"

"Yes."

"Yes, I'm familiar with that."

"Would you agree then that rehabilitation, and not *vindictive justice*, should be the standard by which this Court makes judgments of this nature?"

"I feel that there are several standards to be met in a case like this, and punishment is one of them…rehabilitation is one, punishment is one, uh, the impact on society. There are several standards I would use in a situation like this."

"Okay, so you feel that there should be things added to the Constitution?"

"I think…I think most judges recognize punishment as a legitimate aim of the judicial system"

"Okay, I was asking your opinion. Do you feel that punishment should be added, even though the Constitution says that the principle should be reprimation, not *vindictive justice?*"

That's twice the prosecutor has used the term *vindictive justice.*

"If it is not there, I think it should be, yes."

"I have no further questions."

"Mr. Fleming."

"What was your name again, sir?"

"Bob Bryan."

"Mr. Bryan, have you written editorials of this nature before?"

"No, I have not."

"Is this the first one you've ever done?"

"Yes. Well, wait a minute, I have written editorials frequently. This is the first time, uh, one of this nature has been written."

"What do you mean one of this nature?"

"Uh, one urging the Judge not to accept a plea bargain."

"Do you think that's appropriate journalism?"

"I think if it were...I think if it were used frequently, we would be setting ourselves up as a...as a Superior Court, passing on each decision and that's not our function. I think in a rare instance where a plea bargain seems patently bad, it's appropriate."

"Wouldn't your alternative be to come to court like you're doing right now and tell the Judge about it, rather than writing about it in the newspaper?"

"No, I don't think we're...we're...The newspaper is not an equal party to this business, and we would not expect to be called to pass on the legitimacy of each plea bargain that comes down the pike, no."

"Did you talk with anyone at the Probation Department about this case?"

"No."

"Did you ever talk to Adam Mitchell?"

"No."

"Any members of his family?"

"No."

"Any members of the Lather family?"

"No."

"You base your opinions and your recommendations solely on your own personal opinions then, I assume?"

"I...immediately after the hearing, October 12th, I had a conversation with Mr. Grund about his understanding of the plea bargaining."

"Well, I assume Mr. Grund did not tell you to write this article, urging the Judge not to accept the plea bargain?"

What was Grund doing discussing this case with a reporter?

"No. As far as I know, he had no knowledge of it."

"Do you plan to make this a practice in the future, writing editorials about cases that haven't been decided?"

"No, um, I think we ought to retain that opinion in the rarest of instances, but no, we don't intend to make a practice of it."

"Was the article meant to bring pressure on the Judge in this case?"

"Uh, pressure is too strong of a word. I was...We were expressing our opinion."

"Well, surely the newspaper, writing such things as this, would tend to bring pressure, would it not?"

"If...in...in the general sense of the word pressure, I suppose you could say that this was intended to bring pressure."

"Influence the Judge?"

"Yes, it was."

"You don't think that's an abuse of your fifth amendment, or your first amendment right to free speech in the press?"

"No."

"You didn't compare this case to any others, did you?"

"No."

"Did you do any research on other cases of similar facts and similar crimes?"

"Well, when I said did I compare it, I thought you were talking about in the editorial itself. No, I did not draw comparisons to other cases in the editorial."

"Did you do it before you wrote the editorial?"

"I was aware of several recent sentencings on the third floor of the courthouse here which seemed disproportionate uh…in this particular case."

"How about this particular offense, Reckless Homicide? Did you check anything, any records from this county or surrounding counties, or around the state of Indiana to determine what the usual sentence is for Reckless Homicide?"

"No, I did not."

"When you wrote this editorial, had Mr. Atwell down in Indianapolis been sentenced? Are you familiar with his case?"

"Atwell?"

"Yes."

"I don't think I am."

"Convicted of two counts of Reckless Homicide. He was a Sheriff's Deputy."

"Oh, yes, I had forgotten who he is."

"Did you compare this case, for example, to that case?"

"No, I did not."

"That's all, Judge."

Why didn't Fleming mention that Atwell only received a six-month suspended sentence?

Mr. Grund rose and began cross-examination of the witness.

"Mr. Bryan, since you are now present here in court and have the right to fully and freely express your opinions to the Court, do you have anything else that you feel should be brought to the Court's attention; or any other opinion that you have that you would like to express publicly?"

"Um, I think the thing that surprised me about the reaction to this editorial is that we apparently have far more influence than I thought we did. You would have thought I'd brought this down carved in stone from a mountain. It was simply an expression of an opinion. I thought perhaps it might be an expression of public opinion in this case. Judge, you're going to hear from the probation officer, you're going to hear from parents and from the wife of the deceased. Here, also, is our opinion for what it's worth. There was one other piece of background in this information. I mean in this instance. Over the years we have done what we could at the Tribune editorially to dispel some of this...this...really, this uninformed antagonism toward plea bargaining. We have editorialized that, don't go around tarring the practice of plea bargaining, because plea bargaining is necessary and can be a fine tool of the system. Try to distinguish between good plea bargains and bad plea bargains, and that was the spirit in which we made our comments in this case. That's all I have to say."

"In all other instances, your comments have occurred after the sentencing, however, rather than before, if you were referring to a particular case. Is that correct?"

"I think I would be hard pressed to remember a time when we expressed an opinion after a case. One thing that people very often misunderstand about newspapers is that letters to the editor, which come in after a particular sentence, don't necessarily reflect the opinion of the Tribune. They are simply the opinion of the person who wrote the letter. Now in this particular instance, in addition to the editorial, there was a very nasty letter to the Editor in this case. We didn't necessarily subscribe to the opinions of the letter. But, um, there has been…"

"Are you referring to my letter, which hasn't been put in?" Mr. Grund asked.

"No, no, there was…"

The Judge spoke. "There was one other, name withheld struck in my mind."

"There was a name withheld letter, um, in this particular instance. No, I wasn't referring to your letter, Jim."

"That has not, that reply has never been printed either, is that correct?"

"We are waiting for that one…we are…as far as we're concerned, the ball is in your court now in that."

"I'm saying the reply has never been printed?" Mr. Grund stated.

"Your letter has not been printed."

"You have received my reaction, but you have not printed it?"

"Not at this time."

"That's correct. I have nothing further."

"You may step down. Any other witnesses to call, Mr. Grund?"

"No, Judge."

"Mrs. Lather, do you wish to say anything to the Court at this time?"

"No, Sir."

"And you are Mr. and Mrs. Lather? Is there anything you would like to say to the Court at this time."

My heart was heavy for the parents and widow of Trooper Lather. They appeared to be very nice people. Their faces were drawn from grief, and I could see compassion in them whenever I caught their eyes. I wanted to reach out to them and tell them how sorry I was that this accident had taken place. God must have a special love for parents who have compassion, as they appeared to possess.

"No, Sir."

"Mr. Fleming, do you have any witnesses to call?"

"No, Judge."

"I want to go back to the plea agreement for just a moment. Adam, do you under...I want to make sure you understand this completely. It is my intention, if I accept this plea agreement, that for a period of two-and-a -half years with credit given for the sixty days you've served, and that's the same period of time you'd serve if I just shipped you to the Department of Corrections, do you understand? That for two-and-a-half years, the Court *will* control your placement, and that it will either be in an in-patient facility or in a Department of Corrections facility or in the Miami County Jail. Do you understand that?"

"Yes."

"All right. It's my understanding that the St. Vincent's Stress Center will probably release you quickly, within the next month at least."

"No, I'm not really sure when they're going to."

"Well, the tenor of their report to the probation department would indicated that. It's my intention you should be released to the Sheriff of Miami County, for transportation to the Reception-Diagnostic Center at the Department of Corrections. When you are released from there, you will be brought back to the Miami County jail until we determine what placement is going to be made. Upon completion of that stay, you will serve the balance of the two-and-a-half year period in jail. Do you understand that...or in a Department of Corrections facility?"

"We understand that to be a possibility, Judge, yes."

"I just want to make sure he completely understands this. This is not going to be a situation where the Queen Treatment Facility is your home for a few weeks."

"I understand."

"All right. As a practical matter, you will not be home for two-and-a-half years. None. Do you understand that?"

"Yes."

"Your Honor, so there is no misunderstanding on our part, it's our understanding that the Court would control his placement for five years. The maximum that the Court could actually have him in an in-patient or incarceration would be two-and-a-half years as a result of the law, but he would actually be under the control of the Court for five years."

"If he were in a treatment facility, the court could keep him there for up to five years."

"I simply wanted that clear for the records."

"And, unless I miss my guess, there's going to be a substantial period of this two-and-a-half years that will be spent either in the jail or in a Department of Corrections facility. I want you to understand that completely.

"Yes, sir."

"Okay. Are there any matters in the pre-sentence investigation that need to be gone over at this point?"

"No, Judge," Fleming said.

"No, your honor," replied Mr. Grund.

"Mrs. Lather, I note that in your statement to the probation department, you were not satisfied with the plea agreement. But, if I read this correctly, you don't think the law really provides adequately for this situation?"

"That's right."

"Do you have any misgivings you wish to express about the agreement as we've discussed it today?"

"No, sir."

"All right, any other matters either counsel wants to bring to the Court's attention?"

"No, your Honor."

"Is your time right on the credit time so far…sixty…what did you say?" asked Mr. Fleming.

"He spent sixty days in the Miami County Jail."

"The exact number of days may not be correct, but it's someplace in that area," said Mr. Grund.

"Uh, released from jail on the 24th or 25th of August. He would have been incarcerated on July the 6th," said Ms. Monaghan.

"A little less than sixty days. Now, let's clarify this as well. This placement at St. Vincent's has been done by his family and is being paid for by his family. Is that correct?" the Judge asked.

"Yes, sir," Adam answered.

"And what about subsequent placements? Has that been discussed at all? Uh…the Evansville Treatment facility?"

"The cost at Evansville is anywhere from $11.00 a day to $26.00 a day, based on the family income," answered Ms. Monaghan.

"Is that something that the family intended to pay?" the Judge asked as he looked at me.

"I don't see that I have a choice," I answered but I don't understand how he can be tried as an adult but the family is held financially responsible.

"Okay. If, in fact, that's where he winds up being sent. I would indicate that the Court will not accept a juvenile placement. There was one discussed where the residential arrangement would have been in foster care, and I don't think that's appropriate. This will have to be an in-patient type of facility or a secured type of facility, one or the other. All right, with the clarification we've gotten to the plea agreement and the Court's ability to modify it, the Court will accept the terms of the plea agreement and will withdraw the conditional acceptance of the guilty plea and accept the plea; withdraw the conditional finding of guilty, and enter a finding of guilty, pursuant to the terms of the agreement. Adam, is there anything you'd like to say to the Court before the Court enters the sentence?"

"No, sir."

"The court will sentence according to the terms of the plea agreement; that is, you are sentenced to the Indiana Department of Corrections for a period of five years. That sentence will be suspended. You will be placed on probation for a period of five years, with the terms and conditions as set forth in the plea agreement. Are there any other matters we need to take up at this time?"

Mr. Grund interrupted, "I believe it would be appropriate for the Court simply to return him to St. Vincent's with an order that he then be placed in the custody of the sheriff at such a time as he is released from St. Vincent's."

"We will order St. Vincent's to release him only to the Miami County Sheriff, and we'll direct the sheriff to transport him at his first convenience, after release, to the Reception-Diagnostic Center. Order that a report be filed with the Court, and the Court will at that time determine."

"I need a release of the bail money then, Judge, please."

"Show the bail released at this time. The Court retains a $50.00 administration fee out of the cash bond, and the balance will be returned. Would you notify the Clerk that they can release the bond money. Court costs will need to be paid. Then we'll show pursuant to the agreement, the charges of Driving While Intoxicated and Resisting Law Enforcement are hereby…"

Mr. Grund interrupted again, "The Court didn't waive those. They remained in the juvenile cause."

"Part of your plea agreement was that they be dismissed."

"They actually will be dismissed in the Juvenile Case, then?"

"We'll dismiss them, but they'll be dismissed under the Juvenile Case number, which was J-62-82s. Now, Adam, I want you to understand why the Court is sentencing as it is, or as it has in this case. First of all, at your age, a flat out sentence to the Department of Corrections would probably do nothing but guarantee us that when you are released, we'd see you again, or somebody would. The crime you committed is a very serious one. A life has been lost, and I think you understand the impact of what's happened. But make no mistake about it, if you violate the rules of the Court, I will ship you to the Department of Corrections. Do you understand that?"

"Yes, sir."

"I'm giving you an opportunity. Number one, you're going to serve, if serve is the correct word, the same amount of time you would if you were sentenced to the Department of Corrections for a period of five years. That is, you will be out of your home, your liberty will be restricted, and you will be in someone's custody for that period of time. The difference is, we're going to try to do something constructive. I have no faith in the Department of Corrections doing anything to affect change. They have virtually no programs, even though they say they do. I don't know of anything they could do that would help you, and we're attempting to help. At the same time, make no mistake about it, this sentence is intended to include punishment. One thing you have to learn as an adult is that when you commit a reckless act, there's a price to pay. You have to learn that, and it's a statement that this Court makes to the public in the course of the sentencing, as well. You cannot engage in this kind of conduct, even though you did not intend that a death occur, and get away with it. There is punishment. Reckless conduct will be punished, as will intentional conduct. If this were an intentional killing, you'd be charged with murder and we'd be looking at thirty to sixty years. The fact that you did not intend to kill anyone causes this to be criminal recklessness, but it doesn't do a thing for Mr. Lather's family. I only hope that when this is all over, we are going to see Adam Mitchell being a productive adult; and that's one of the reasons we are attempting to do what we're doing. Okay. Anything further?"

"No, your Honor."

"We will adjourn."

# Chapter 11

Adam was released from St. Vincent's hospital after Thanksgiving and sent back to the Peru jail.

I was making one of my weekly trips on Sunday to see Adam and take him some money. "Would you see to it that Adam Mitchell gets this money? And I'll need a receipt, too," I said to the policeman that was on duty.

"We aren't thieves here. He'll get his money."

"I wasn't calling you a thief. I guess I don't know who to trust after this case with my son. I have this awful feeling that everyone is against us."

"If you're talking about that article that Bob Bryan put in the paper, it wasn't about your son. It was about the Judge's friends getting away with drunk driving and the ordinary citizen getting threaded differently."

"I appreciate you sharing that with me."

No comment. I guess he decided he had said too much. He called Adam's name for a visitor and I was let into the visiting room.

"Don't hug me, Mom. You're not supposed to touch the inmates. They try to smuggle drugs into the jail and you're not supposed to touch us. I don't want anyone thinking my Mom would do that."

"Wow, sounds like you're learning a lot in here."

"Not really. The people who run this place are very nice to me. They have been having church services and I met the Chief's wife. She's a really great lady. She told me that she knows Grandma Mitchell."

"I know. Grandma called me and told me the same thing. Your grandmother knows the police chief's wife. I guess she comes in here and visits with the inmates. Anyway, she told Grandma that you didn't belong in jail and she said you're not jail material."

"I wish I could do all of my time here. They really are nice to me."

"I would like that, too, but I'm afraid that's not going to happen. You know Christmas is coming up. Do you know of anything that I could get you that you can have here."

"There a book called *The Book*. People in here are talking about it and I'd like to have it. There's not much to do except read."

"Then I'll get it for you. Anything else?"

"I don't know if I could have it, but I get so cold and it would be nice to have a vest to keep me warm."

"You are getting thinner everytime I see you. You need to eat more."

"I eat everything they bring me. The sheriff's wife does the cooking and it's always good. I just don't get enough of it." He paused, then changed subjects.

"Mom, I met a girl in here. She's really talented. She makes cards for people and she's a great artist. She was being pulled over for speeding and because she didn't have a license she tried to outrun the police. She and another girl got in a fight and now she's in here for attempted murder. It really wasn't her fault. The other girl pushed her into it. She stabbed her with a pair of scissors. The other girl isn't hurt that bad. But, Mom, what I was wondering is if you would cut her hair for her for Christmas? We would have to get permission from the sheriff, but I know he would let you do that for her for Christmas. Please, Mom."

"Adam, if you want me to do that for her, I'll be glad to. You make the arrangements and I'll bring my scissors."

"Visiting time is over," came the intercom voice.

"Adam, take care of yourself and remember I love you very much."

"Love you, too, Mom, and thanks for doing that for me. She'll be surprised and it'll make her happy."

I was hearing what the policeman said, going over and over again in my mind, confirming my gut feeling that there was a lot more to this case than met the eye. I just didn't know how to prove it.

# Chapter 12

Clay was sitting at the dining room table when I came home from work. "Do you have a few minutes to talk?" he asked.

I sat my purse on a chair and took a seat across the table from him.

"I've been thinking. This isn't working. I was wondering if you could find a place for me, a small house that might need some work, that I could move into. It would give me something to do."

I had hoped that what he wanted was to apologize and tell me how much he really loved me, but, no, he just needed my services again.

"I'll help you find a place, Clay."

I missed an opportunity to forgive Clay and ask him not to move out, but I guess my anger outweighed my love for him at that time. I didn't even think about it until it was too late.

I located a place on the west side of town at the edge of the park where I had first met Clay on the 4th of July that had brought us together. Clay liked the house. He made an offer on it. It seemed strange to have my husband as a client. Seeing Clay move out of our home upset me tremendously. I had mixed feelings about Clay, and now I felt abandoned in a physical way. Before, Clay had been still in the house and I saw him. Now he was gone and I was alone. I had no one to care for me, and no one to cook for. I felt totally isolated in the Cape Cod home that I had loved so dearly.

Adam stayed at the jail in Peru until the middle of January when they moved him to the Genesis House in Marion, Indiana. He called me on the phone.

"Mom, you have to get me out of this place. It's filthy and the cook is drunk most of the time. They do drugs here. How am I supposed to go to school over here and live like this? This place is horrible."

"I'll call Jim and see what can be done about moving you. Just do what you know is right and keep your chin up. It's going to be okay. I'll be over on Sunday and we'll go to church together."

I called Jim Fleming immediately. "Jim, I just got a call from Adam. He says the place they have put him is filthy and the cook is drunk most of the time. Can you get him moved to a better place?"

"Paige, take my word on this. *Leave it alone.* He is as well off there as anywhere he can be. He'll have to adjust."

"I don't know how the courts expect an immature 18 year old to rise above his problems when he has been placed in an environment like Adam has described."

"Like I said, *leave it alone,*" Jim repeated.

"Sure, Jim…sure."

Now the "leave it alone" in Jim's voice began playing like a broken record in my mind. What was going on with this case that I didn't know about? And, more importantly, how was I going to find out what it was?

I went to Marion on Sunday and took my camera with me. The place was worse than Adam had described. Even the linens on the beds were filthy. There were beer bottles everywhere and the place smelled so badly, I could hardly stay in there to take pictures. I returned to Kokomo and called Clay.

"Oh, Clay, I just came back from Marion and the halfway house that Adam is in is horrible. It's filthy and Adam said the cook is drunk half of the time and doesn't cook like he was supposed to. I was wondering if you would take Adam's bed and clean sheets over there so at least he could have a clean place to sleep. I'll send some food, too."

"Sure. No problem." Clay surprised me by agreeing to do it. I felt better about where Adam laid his head at night, but I was always thinking about what Jim had said.

Months passed and I was faithful about seeing Adam every Sunday. We would go to church and spend the rest of our time together at the mall or just driving around. Once in awhile I would drive Adam back home for a few hours.

Jenny went to see him, too, and he was always in a better mood after one of her visits.

The phone was ringing. I looked at the clock. One thirty in the morning. I wondered who might be calling at this hour as I picked up the phone.

"Mom, a man broke in here and tried to rape me!" Adam sounded hysterical.

"Are you okay?"

"Yes, I think so." His voice sounded like he was trying to stop crying, "I just want out of here, Mom."

"Listen to me, Adam, can you go to your room and lock the doors?"

"Mom, there aren't locks on the inside doors."

I felt so helpless. "Adam, if everything is under control, do you feel safe enough to try to go back to sleep? Things will look better in the morning."

"I'll try, Mom, but please, try to get me out of here."

"I'll see what I can do." I hung up the phone, got out of bed and called the Marion Police Department. "This is the mother of Adam Mitchell and he is at a halfway house there in Marion. He just called me and told me that a man broke into the house and tried to rape him."

"What halfway house is it?" the officer asked.

"It's called the Genesis House."

"What is your son in there for?"

"He hit and killed someone in a car accident," I said.

"Lady, I don't care what he did, that place is bad news. You need to get him out of there."

"I called you so that this would be an official report and I would have proof of the things that are going on over there," I said.

"It's an official report, but if you love your son get him out of there," The officer said.

I tried to go back to sleep, but it was no use. I was in such a state that I couldn't close my eyes. I kept thinking of what Jim had said, *"Just leave it alone."* I wondered why he would say such a thing. If it was *his* son if he would leave *it alone*? It seemed to me that the court system should know what kind of a place it is using to place troubled young people. I also thought of other things: first there were witnesses and then there weren't; then *the results would be the same* to ask for a change of venue. Now it's *leave it alone*. There was something that wasn't being disclosed or there was a reason that Jim was taking this kind of an attitude. I tossed and turned and at first light I got out of bed.

I waited for 9:00 so I could call Jim's office. I explained the call from Adam and also the conversation with the police officer in Marion. I got the same answer.

"Paige, I know how frustrating this is for you. But there is nothing that can be done. If he messes up over there, they are going to send him to prison. You're going to have to find a way to live with it."

"I don't know how you expect me to live with it." I hung up the phone and sat down and cried. *Why can't I help my son when he is in such a filthy, despicable place?* My heart was breaking and Jim was right, in a way I did have to find a way to live with this or else I would lose my mind.

I couldn't *leave it alone.* I thought about Diane Monahan, Adam's case worker. It was her job to find a suitable place for the court to place Adam. I wondered if she had even gone to the halfway house before the court had sent him over there.

Months passed and both of us were doing our best to adjust and *leave it alone.* Adam had his fill, and no matter how supportive I tried to be it wasn't working. Adam was going to AA meetings, but he only found new people with problems to drink with.

# Chapter 13

It was late summer, and Adam had decided that jail was better than living in such a filthy place. He called Diane Monahan.

"Miss Monahan, this is Adam Mitchell and I need to tell you something."

"Yes, Adam, go ahead."

"Well, I've tried since I've been in this place and I can't take it any more. I've been drinking. I haven't been for the last couple of week, but I just can't take this place anymore."

"Of course, you know this means you will go back to jail."

"I know, but it's better than *this* place. Have you ever been in this halfway house?" Adam asked.

"No, Adam, I haven't. It's my job to locate the places that are available," Diane said.

It was the next day that the police showed up to take Adam back to jail.

I went to see my son in Peru at the jail as soon as they would allow me to. The place looked all too familiar as I was led back to the room provided for visiting.

"How are they treating you here? Adam."

"It's not bad. The sheriff's wife comes in sometimes. I really like her. It's not that bad here, Mom. It's better than the halfway house. Oh, I asked Diane Monahan if she had ever been in the Genesis house and she said she hadn't."

"See what I mean, Adam? If I were running a court that placed people in a facility, I would know something about the facility. I wouldn't send an emotional person of any kind to a place like the Genesis House and expect him to overcome problems when the place itself is a problem. I wonder how many people really get any kind of help from our so-called judicial system," I said.

"There's talk that they might send me to Central State Hospital for an evaluation and drug and alcohol treatment."

"I don't have a problem with that Adam. It'll do you good to have some professional help."

"Mom, I don't know why I drink. Judge Embrey is having one of his friends pick me up and take me to an AA meeting."

"Well, that sounds like he is trying to help or has a lot of friends in AA. I wonder if the Judge knows that the Probation Officer has never been in the Genesis house? I can understand where the phrase Blind Justice comes from. They put on blinders and make motions so everybody will think they are trying their best to help people."

"Mom, try not to worry about me. I'm going to be okay! I'm better off here than at the Genesis House. At least here I get three meals a day and I can sleep without worrying who is coming after me. Please, Mom, try to stop worrying. I'll be all right."

"I'm sorry, Adam. I guess I'm at the end of my rope. I feel completely frustrated. I know as well as I know my own name that there is something being covered up here, and I don't know how to go about uncovering it."

"Mom, I'll just do my time and it will be over with sooner. Please, don't worry about me. Look at it this way: I can't drink in here."

"You're got a point there."

"Mom, I really would like to spend all of my time right here in Peru."

"It would be nice, but I don't think that's going to happen.  We'll just take it one day at a time. Visiting hours is almost up so I need to get going. I'll be back next Sunday. I love you."

"Remember Mom! No, worrying. I love you too."

# Chapter 14

Adam had been sent to Central State hospital for an evaluation. It was during his short stay there that my Daddy had called.

"Hi, honey, how's things going?"

"I guess things are about the same. Only time is going to change anything," I said.

"Your Mama wants us to come to Indiana to see you and Adam."

"That's great, Daddy. When are you coming up?'

"When is a good time for you?"

"Anytime is fine for me, but Adam can't have visitors except on Sundays."

"Well, then, we'll be there by the middle of the week and we can spend some time with you before we go to see Adam."

"Daddy, I'm so happy you're coming here, I can hardly wait to see you both."

"I'll call again and let you know about what time to expect us, okay?"

"Okay, Daddy. Give Mama a kiss for me."

I was thrilled. I felt like a little girl who had missed her parents more than she'd realized. I was more anxious to see my mother and see how she was getting along. The days passed slowly and my parents finally arrived. Mother was walking with a walker and was still paralyzed on the left side. She had her arm in a sling to keep it from just hanging. I was saddened by the appearance of Mama. It was a totally different look from before her stroke. She had kept her jet-black hair pulled back with combs and she was always tanned from the time she spent working in her flowerbeds. It was obvious that she was part Indian. She had a lively spirit about her and always dressed in bright colors. Now, as I looked at Mama, the lively spirit was gone and it was an effort for her to use the walker. Before, her clothes added color to her golden skin, but now her clothes seem to hang on her and she was dragging one foot.

Shaking off what I was seeing, I ran to her, gave her a hug, and welcomed her to my home. I helped Daddy get Mama up the three steps into the kitchen and then led her into the living room and sat her in the chair that I nestled myself in every evening. It was cushy and I wanted her to be as comfortable as possible. I put their things in my bedroom on the main floor. I would sleep in the guest room.

"Hungry? Can I get you something to drink?"

"We just had lunch, but I'll take a cup of coffee if you have it."

"I'll make a fresh pot for you, Mama. Daddy would you like some, too?"

"Yeah, I'll have a cup."

From the kitchen I called, "Did you have a good trip?"

"It wasn't bad. We just took our time. It was really pretty coming through the mountain." My father answered.

"Mama, did you enjoy the trip?"

"Yes, I've always enjoyed coming through the mountains. I like going 441 up through Cherokee, but it takes a lot longer and we weren't sure how I would do on a long trip."

"Every once in a while we would stop and I would help her get into the back of the camper and she would rest for a while and then I'd stop and help her back up front so she

143

could see better. We can drive the camper to Indianapolis to see Adam if you want to."

"I'll be fine. It's not that far, I can ride in your car."

"Paige, I hope you don't mind, but I would really like to see Clay while we're here. Do you know where he lives?" my mother asked.

"Of course I know where he lives. It's kind of funny. He lives within a half a block of where we first met. Remember the 4th of July when you were here and we went to a picnic with some of the people he worked with. If it wasn't for the trees, he could stand on his front porch and look down on the very spot that we met."

Fearing the tears might come I continued, "I sold him a small home over by Highland Park and he's remodeling it. I stop by to see him every once in a while. Wait until you see it. He's done a nice job. The one thing that struck me funny was, you remember the truck I bought him that he was so proud of? Remember we went to the dealership and I told him to pick out anything that he wanted on the truck and he wanted an orange truck? Well, his counter tops in the kitchen are orange. Once when I was over there we were talking and he said he was so glad that he didn't have knots in his bread wrappers any more. He leaves the dish soap out on the counter, too. He never said a word to me about tying knots in the bread wrappers when we were married, and I guess he didn't like the liquid dish soap under the counter either. I must have irritated him pretty bad, Mama." I felt somewhat ashamed that my parents had had such a long marriage, yet I had failed so miserably with men.

"I thought I was a good wife, and now I hear he didn't like knots in his bread wrappers. I wonder what else I did that made him move out when I needed him more than ever."

"Honey, don't worry, if you're supposed to get back together it will happen. The Lord works in mysterious ways. Best thing to do now is leave him alone."

"I know he'll be glad to see you and Daddy. We'll stop by there tomorrow after he gets off work."


Clay was working outside when we arrived. He smiled when he saw my parents. He came over to the car immediately and helped Mama get out. I let them talk and tried to stay out of Clay's view.

"Come on in and we'll have some iced tea," Clay insisted.

I watched as Clay brought the iced tea to each of them.

The visit was awkward and a dead silence filled the room. I couldn't stand it. I broke the awkward silence with, "Mama and Daddy came up to see Adam, and they wanted to see you too, while they were here."

"I'm glad you stopped by. It's been awhile. How long has it been? A couple of years, I really can't remember."

"I was telling Mama what a nice job you've done on your house."

"I've got a lot more work to do. It's slow going when I can only work on it after work every day." No one spoke, so Clay continued talking.

"Paige tells me you've really been having a rough time since you had your stroke."

Mama nodded her agreement. "It was really hard in the beginning. They shaved my head and now my hair is grown out enough so that I'm gonna have Paige fix it for me while

I'm here. We're going to see Adam on Sunday. I don't want to scare him to death." She smiled and rubbed her head.

"It doesn't look that bad. Anybody want any more tea?"

"No, thank you. We need to get going. Mama and Daddy just wanted to see you while they are here and I know you're busy, so we need to get going," I said.

"Thanks for the tea." Daddy said as he shook Clay's hand. Daddy had always liked Clay. They had a lot in common and were very comfortable around each other. "You have a nice home here, if you ever get back down South stop in to see us. It was good to see you, Clay."

"Thanks for coming to see me, Clay said. After we were in the car I asked Mama,"What did you think of his orange countertop?" I asked my mother.

"You know me, Paige I kind of liked it. Of course I like bright colors."

"Well, I guess it's better than red!" I was smiling at my mother, knowing her favorite color was red.


It was September and the days were bright and crisp. The garden was at the end of its season and it was a time to prepare for the coming winter. My parents were impressed with the huge garden that I had and were enjoying the fruits of my labor. The collards were as pretty as any my mother had every seen.

"You need to pick some of these collards and cook them for your Daddy. He loves collards and black-eyed peas."

"I can do that. In fact I have some peas frozen. We'll have them for supper tonight. You know, Mama, people up here don't say supper. They have lunch and then dinner. At home we have dinner and then supper. I get a lot of kidding over the way I talk. I guess the best one was the time I was helping my friend Carol cook and I asked if she had any handling rags, and she didn't have a clue what I was talking about. They call them potholders in Indiana. The 850 miles between here and Georgia is like being in a different country. Funny thing, though, you should hear them say words like Piano, Galveston, Peru they pronounce then PIE-an-no, GAL—vest-ton and PEErue, and they think I talk funny." I had my mother laughing and it was music to my ears.

"Paige, you remind me of when you were little, always coming home with a new joke. Some of them you had no idea what you were telling, but because people laughed you just kept telling one right after another."

"I'm embarrassed to say that I have thought about one of those jokes and I've never told that one again."

Sunday arrived and the moment Adam saw his grandmother he smiled and seemed happy. They had always been close and Adam used to love to spend his summers with Grandma and Grandpa. Adam had accompanied his Grandma to her ceramic classes and gotten interested in doing it himself. They had spent hours together one summer doing ceramic frogs that held scratchy pads to use when doing the dishes. My ceramic frog sat on one corner of my kitchen sink as a constant reminder of Adam and happier days.

Adam thanked God that he was at a hospital for Grandma and Grandpa's visit. He would have hated for them to see him while he was in prison. Somehow it was easier for him to face them while he was at Central State

Hospital, and no one asked the exact details of why he was there. It was easier to say that he wasn't coping well and let it go at that. The truth of why he was there might never be told in words that could be heard. Somehow, if it stayed silent then it wasn't a part of reality, except to Adam.

"When you get out are you coming back to Tybee to live?" Grandma asked.

"You bet. I'm living for that day, Grandma. I'll come down there and help take care of you," Adam said.

"I'll be glad to get a break," Grandpa chimed in.

No one asked any questions. We just made small talk to keep things on a cheerful note for Adam's sake. We didn't have to be brain surgeons to see that being in prison was taken a toll on Adam.

While I was glad to see my parents, I was very worried about my mother. The stroke had definitely taken most of the spark out of her and I was saddened by what I witnessed during their visit. Mama had always been the caregiver, but now their roles had switched. Daddy was taking care of Mama, and it didn't appear that Mama was any better than the last time I had seen her.

When we ended our visit Adam hugged my mother so long, I was afraid he might never let go. It was then I realized how homesick, frightened and lost he was feeling.

# Chapter 15

I was raking leaves when Clay pulled into the driveway. I walked toward his truck.

"Hi, there," he called out, waving.

"What are you doing in this part of town?" I asked.

"I just drove over to see if you would like to go deer hunting with me next week."

"Are you serious, Clay?"

"Yes, I'm serious. I know you like to deer hunt and I thought you might like to go."

"I really would. It would be fun. When are you leaving?"

"I thought we could leave right after I get off work on Friday. Just like we used to."

"Okay, I'll be ready. Do you need for me to take anything special?"

"No, I'll have the camper packed. I'll pick you up about 3:30 next Friday."

Clay put his truck in reverse and started to back away. I couldn't believe he wanted me to go deer hunting with him. I felt like a schoolgirl going on her first date.

I put down my rake, went into the house and called Carol to share my good news.

"Hi, Carol, I'm so excited. Clay asked me to go deer hunting with him next week."

"What did you tell him?"

"What do you think I told him? I told him I would go with him. Carol I've missed him so much and I'm really hoping we can get this worked out between us."

"If that's what you want, Paige, then I'm happy for you. But I don't know that I would want to work things out with him if I were you." Carol said.

"Carol, we had a lot of good years together before this accident and I just think that Clay didn't know what to do. He just moved out so he wouldn't have to deal with all of the problems."

"Yeah, he moved out and let you deal with all of them, while he was out dancing every night and you were home crying your eyes out. Like I said, I wouldn't want to work things out with him if I were you. You are much more understanding that I would ever be with him."

"I know it's hard to understand, but at one time we were so close we could tell what the other one was thinking, and I don't know that I'll ever find another man like Clay."

"I wouldn't want one like Clay! I'm glad I raised my sons by myself instead of having a stepfather around to make things worse. If I had to do it all over, I'd still raise my boys by myself."

"I know Carol. I just want to do this. Maybe it won't work, but at least I can go deer hunting one more time. Besides, I love Colorado in the fall. It's beautiful. The trees are golden and the sky is a brilliant blue. I'll have fun. I'll take lots of pictures so you can see how beautiful it is in Colorado."

"Good luck, Paige. I hope things work out for the best for you. You deserve it."

"Oh, Carol, I'm going to see Adam tomorrow and tell him if anything changes while I'm gone to call you okay? Then I'll check in with you while I'm gone."

"Sure."

"Thanks, Carol. I'll call you. Bye."

It seemed like Friday would never come. I was excited about the trip to Colorado and was pacing the floor when Clay pulled into the driveway. I grabbed my things and headed out to the truck. We were finally on our way to Colorado together.

We had been deer hunting many times together, and it was comfortable being with Clay.

The first evening in the camper Clay leaned over and kissed me goodnight. It was a beginning I thought. Maybe this trip will be a turning point for us.

We finally reached Montrose, Colorado and parked the fifth wheel on the property that we had owned together and Clay had gotten in the divorce. The last time I had been at that property my Mother and Father had gone to Colorado with us. Daddy had to be put in the hospital while we were there. Mama had gotten sick too. The doctor told us Daddy had pneumonia and that he would have to be on oxygen for awhile. He could be released in a few days and that we needed to take him out of the high altitude as soon as we could and for him not to ever come back to Colorado. It was during Daddy's recovery after he was back on Tybee that Mama had had her stroke.

Now, here I was again deer hunting with Clay. The memories of the previous years hanging in my head like pictures on a wall.

One came to mind in particular. We were first starting out with our deer hunting years before. We had been hunting all morning and the coolness of the morning had been replaced with the warm dry sunny noontime. The sky was a brilliant blue and the Aspens were golden. We were both ready to start taking off some of our clothes. It was so peaceful in the woods and the silence had it's own nature sounds singing in the background. I moved close to Clay, "What do you say we take off a few more clothes and make love in the woods?"

"Are you nuts? We can't do that!"

"Who says we can't?"

"I say we're not going to!"

It added one more rejection to my already monumental collection of rejections. I thought about that now and wondered if Clay had any intention of getting personal on this trip. I know my reject bag was about full and I couldn't make any moves that would get me anymore of the worthless feeling. I'd just have to remember all of the nights when the train's whistle would sound, and wake us, and Clay would want to make love. Oh, how, sweet it had been in the beginning.

I called Carol after several days.

"Hey. Have you heard from Adam?"

"Yes. He called two days ago and said they were taking him from Central State to a halfway house in Fort Wayne. He said he would call with an address and phone number after he got there. How's you trip?"

"Well, it's not what I had hoped. But, I'm trying to enjoy it. Probably the last time I'll ever be able to go deer hunting in Colorado. I'll call you when I get home. How did Adam sound when you talked to him?"

"I thought he sounded good. Billy talked to him for a few minutes and he thought he sounded good too."

"Thanks Carol. I'll call you when I get home."

# Chapter 16

Adam had been in the Fort Wayne facility for only a short time. It was the day after Thanksgiving when I got a call that he had been brought back to the Peru Jail. He had been drinking again. I went to see him on Sunday.

"Hi, Mom, Sorry about this. I don't know why I did it. I know how much this has cost you. Now that I'm nineteen, I want to ask the court to appoint an attorney for me."

"I think that's a good idea. I don't understand much about the law, but it seems strange to me. Maybe you can find one who will have more to say than *leave it alone*. You do what you feel is best. I'm not sure that this case was right from the start. I'm still confused on how they could try you as an adult, but hold us responsible financially as your parents."

"Me either, Mom."

"Adam, I've done all I know to do for you. We'll do it your way. Lord knows, my way hasn't worked out right. Get yourself an attorney."

I left the jail feeling like my son was becoming my support system. It was late November and the gray sky made me want to go south. It looked like I would be spending another Christmas Day at the Peru Jail.

A hearing was set for the judge to make another decision in Adam's case. The bailiff said, "All Rise. Be it remembered, on the 6th day of December 1983, the same being Calendar Year 1983, the above and foregoing cause of action came to be heard before the Honorable Bruce C. Embrey, sole judge of the Miami County Superior Court.

Judge Embrey said, "This is Case Number F-33-82S, State of Indiana versus Adam A. Mitchell. Mr. Mitchell, would you be seated at the counsel table, please. The sentencing in this matter took place on the 1$^{st}$ day of November 1982. There have been a series of placements, the most recent of which was at the 13$^{th}$ Step House in Fort Wayne, Indiana. Mr. Mitchell, it has been reported to this Court that you violated the rules of the 13$^{th}$ Step House by returning from work one evening intoxicated. The issue at this point is whether or not there is any reason why the Court should not proceed to sentence you, under the terms of the plea agreement that were entered by you on the 1$^{st}$ of November, 1982. Are you represented by council at this time?"

"No."

"Do you intend to be?"

"Um, could I be appointed counsel?"

"Why?"

"Because I can't afford it."

"Yeah, but what are you hoping to accomplish at this point? I'm not asking you to admit or deny. Under the terms of the plea agreement, this Court has a total discretion over your life and the place where you're placed for a period of two-and-a-half years. It's not a matter of the State providing anything, Mr. Mitchell. What it is you hope to show this Court?"

"I don't know."

"Is there some reason why the Court should not sentence you in accordance with the terms of the plea agreement?"

"I would like to say something, yes."

"Go ahead."

"I spent a year-and a-half of my life alone. I went through this accident by myself. I woke up a nights crying, and there's no one there for me. That's all I ever wanted of this...was someone to be there to help me through this. And for a year-and-a-half I've tried to get through day by day, and it's not easy. I have something I have to live with for the rest of my life, and it's real hard for me to have to go through that alone. All I ever wanted was to be loved and be with my family, and I'm sorry."

"I would suppose Mrs. Lather probably feels a little lonely at this point, too," responded the Judge. "And I'm sorry if I'm not terribly moved by that speech, Mr. Mitchell, but this Court has bent over backward giving you opportunities to straighten out the problems that you have, and I'm not seeing any progress. We sent you to the Genesis House. You drank and used drugs. We sent you to the 13th Step House, and you came back drunk. Now, *you* tell me where the improvement is, and you tell me who I'm suppose to be sympathetic for at this point."

"I'm trying."

"I don't see much proof of that, quite frankly."

"I quit drinking."

"Really?"

"Yes, I did."

"It's been fairly recent, hasn't it?"

"Yes, that's been one time."

"I think you've been in secure custody since your last drinking episode. I'm not aware...I think there's a real void in the law at this point. I am not certain of whether you have a right to counsel at this point in time. I will let you consult with this Court's Public Defender before

155

pronouncing sentence. The only thing…I don't know what there is to prove or disprove at this point. Under the terms of the plea agreement, this Court has a great deal of discretion. We spent about a half-hour on the record, when I accepted that plea agreement, making sure you, the Prosecutor, and your attorney understood the terms of the agreement. And the agreement gives me an extraordinary amount of discretion in handling the case. Frankly, I'm through attempting rehabilitation with you. This is the third placement that was to be…fourth, actually, that was to be rehabilitative. I don't think we can do much more. So, the issue when we come back here is whether or not there's any good reason why you should not be sent to the Indiana Department of Corrections. If you want to talk with a lawyer to discuss that matter, then I will allow you to discuss it with Mr. Criss. In the meantime, I will remand you to the custody of the Miami County Sheriff. We'll see if we can get this heard next week. Any questions?"

"No."

Adam looked scared as they escorted him out of the courtroom. I wondered if this wasn't just putting off the inevitable. Adam was going to prison.

# Chapter 17

The weather was getting colder and another Christmas was just a couple of weeks away. I hadn't started my Christmas shopping and was secretly wishing I could just skip Christmas. It was obvious that the hearing wouldn't take place until after the holidays and I would probably be able to see Adam on Christmas Day. What could I buy for my son while he was in jail? I couldn't just forget about Clay. He had been my husband for eighteen years and I still loved him even though he didn't seem to love me.

I called Clay. "Hi, it's me and I was wondering if you have any plans for Christmas day?"

"I hadn't thought about it."

"I was wondering if you would consider having dinner here at the house and then going with me to see Adam. I know if I were in jail on Christmas I would want to see my parents."

"I can do that" Clay said.

"Good! I'll have dinner ready at 12:30 and we can drive to Peru together afterward," I said. I was happy that Clay had agreed to eat Christmas dinner with me. I had always heard that the way to a man's heart was through his stomach, and if there was anything that Clay enjoyed it was eating my cooking. I would plan a special meal and make the most of the day.


It seemed extra quiet on Christmas morning, no traffic on the roads covered with freshly fallen snow. It was beautiful outside, but the temperature had dropped below freezing. The ground was wrapped in a white blanket and the trees had a heavy coat of snow on every branch. The sun was shining, and it was almost blinding it was so bright outside.

The phone rang. "Hi, my truck won't start. Looks like I'll have to skip dinner."

"That's not a problem. I'll come and pick you up around noon."

"Okay. I'll keep trying with the truck and if I get it started I'll call you."

"Okay."

I checked the turkey and started preparing a sweet potato pie. I wanted everything to be as delicious as possible. I got the china from the cabinet and set the table for two in the dining room. When everything had been taken care of, I showered and dressed to go after Clay while dinner finished cooking.

Clay was waiting for me when I arrived and I wanted to give him a big hug, but was afraid to. It was Christmas day and I didn't want to do or say anything to spoil Christmas any more than it was already. Visiting your son in jail on Christmas wasn't the most pleasant way to spend Christmas. In years past we had always gone to Clay's mother's home for Christmas, but since the accident it seemed like all family traditions were out the window. I just didn't know what to expect in my life anymore. The only thing I was certain about was that having my son in jail on Christmas was almost more than I could accept and not having Clay's support on a daily basis was making my life worse.

Clay had been looking out the window when I pulled up in front of his house.  In just a few minutes we were on our way.

"I thought for sure my truck would start this morning," he said when he loaded his large frame into the front seat beside me.

"I didn't mind coming after you."

"I hate it when my truck won't run."

I felt the old feeling starting to boil inside me. That truck had always been more important to him than I was.

"I hope you're hungry. I think I've cooked enough for an army."

"I didn't eat any breakfast 'cause I knew I would be having a good dinner." Clay smiled at me.

There were parts of him that I loved desperately.  He had a smile that melted my soul and I had always loved to cook for Clay. I couldn't recall one thing that I had ever cooked for him that he complained about.  Well, wait now, there was the rhubarb cake. I had cut a small piece and taken it to him fresh from the oven.  I put the cake into his mouth and waited for a response. "Well, what do you think?"

"It's pretty good, but it has a different flavor."

"It's rhubarb cake!"

"I told you I don't like rhubarb!"

"I just thought if you didn't know what it was you might like it."

"Well, I don't."  He could be stubborn like that.

He was so comfortable to be with. I had always felt safe with Clay.  I knew he would never let any harm come to me and I relished the safety of his presence.

Christmas dinner was as delicious as I had hoped it would be and Clay enjoyed it. "Did you save room for pie?"

"You bet I did. Is it pumpkin or sweet potato?"

"Sweet potato. You remember what your brother Billy said? 'This is the best pumpkin pie I ever ate.' I'll never forget the look on his face when I told him it was sweet potato and he quit eating the minute I told him. I've always regretted not waiting until he finished the whole slice of pie before I told him it was sweet potato and not pumpkin."

"I guess I'm kinda mean like that," I said.

"You would have thought he would have finished it being as he liked it until he found out what it was." Clay was enjoying himself. It was almost as if nothing was wrong between us.

"Here's a little something for Christmas." I handed him a beautifully wrapped package.

"I didn't get you anything."

Clay, unwrapped the package and smiled as he looked at the new western shirt with pearl snaps, the kind he liked to wear when we used to go square dancing together.

"It's okay. Think we need to get going so we're not late for visitin' hours?"

I picked up the only packages left under the Christmas tree, unplugged the lights, threw on my coat and the two of us headed to Peru to visit Adam.

The routine at the jail was the same. A policeman opened the packages before they were given to Adam.

"I hope you like it," I said as Adam pulled out a small lime green duffle bag with his initials monogrammed on it in dark blue.

"It's great Mom, I'm probably the only guy in jail with a monogrammed bag." He said as his blue eyes sparkled with a big smile on his face.

"I thought it would give you a place to put your things in. It's hard to buy for you right now."

Adam went through the rest of his presents.

"Thank you both. It's kind of weird to say Merry Christmas when you're sitting in jail."

"It'll be different next year. Just remember we're celebrating the birth of Jesus and we need to keep that in mind." *It's hard to think of the right thing to say,* I said to myself. *I'm thankful that your Dad has come to see you and we can spend a few minutes acting like a loving family.*

"I think time is just about up. Some people aren't having anybody come to see them today. I don't know what I would do without you, Mom. You, too, Dad." The tears that he was fighting had his blue eyes glassy and he seemed ashamed to be there.

"Time's up," came a voice from the door.

I gave my son a hug and kissed him on the cheek and Clay reached for him, too. I silently thanked God that Clay had come to see Adam on Christmas.

# **Chapter 18**

I was rather busy after Christmas. Most of the factories are closed for the entire week and it gives couples a chance to look at homes while they are off work.

I was at the office when Carol called.

"Got time for lunch today?"

"I'd love to. What time?"

"I can be there in ten minutes."

"I'll be ready." I wondered what had prompted Carol to call me to have lunch. We had been friends for a long time but we had never done the lunch thing. Something was up.

I was putting my coat on and thinking how I really disliked winter clothes. They are so heavy and I must weight an extra 10 pounds with boots, coats, gloves, scarves, and a hat. "I'll be glad when spring gets here," I said as I got into Carol's car.

"Me, too."

"I could have driven, but I figured your car was already warn. It must be 10 degrees below zero outside."

"It's pretty cold. Where would you like to have lunch?"

"There's a new place in the mall. Want to try it?"

"Good idea. I even have a sweater to return there. That's if you have time?"

"I'm fine. I'm showing a couple of house around two-thirty. I've already picked up the keys, so we have plenty of time."

The mall was almost as busy as before Christmas. People were exchanging gifts and all kinds of sales were going on. I love the hustle and bustle of the holidays with the bell ringers, and the Christmas music gave the air a feeling that Christmas hadn't arrived. The decorations were awesome in the mall and the shoppers were smiling and happy.

We made our way to the small café and joined four other people waiting in line for a table.

"How many?"

"Two," Carol said.

In just a few minutes the young girl returned with two menus and we followed her to a booth in the corner with a view of the shoppers.

"So, what's up, Carol?"

"You're good, aren't you? How did you know something was up?"

"Just an instinct I have. I must have inherited it from my mother. Sometimes I can be thinking about my mom and she will call. Not so much anymore, but before she had her stroke we were always doing that to one another."

"First, I wanted to let you know that my brother, Don, got a year for buying alcohol for the boys. He's getting out next week, but he's not coming back to Kokomo. He's going back to Ohio where we were raised."

"And?"

"This is the hard part. I know this is none of my business, but considering our track record as friends I thought I would ask you. Do you know Jenny is pregnant?"

I looked obviously surprised.

"No, Carol, I didn't know. Are you sure?"

"Well, according to Billy she is. I felt you needed to know. Billy mentioned it to me and I wondered why you hadn't told me."

"Carol, I really appreciate you telling me. Do you know when the baby is due?"

"No, I don't, but the way Billy talks she pretty far along."

"Thank you so much, Carol. I really appreciate you as a friend."

My mind was racing. Why hadn't Adam told me? Maybe Adam didn't know. I thought he would have told me if he knew himself. How could he have not told me? *Maybe this will be the good that comes out of this tragedy,* I told myself. *This will give Adam something to look forward to. I wonder how Jenny is doing?*

The waitress brought our food and we sat there eating and absorbing the news of a new baby. I had been so focused on myself, and Adam, that I hadn't even taken the time to think about Jenny. This is going to be great. A new baby!

"Carol, this is a real shock, but a good one. This could be the very thing that will keep Adam's spirits up for the rest of the time he has left to serve."

"I'm surprised that you're taking it so well," Carol said.

"Surely you haven't forgotten about me being pregnant when I married Clay? I know what it feels like to be ashamed and rejected by your family and friends. I wouldn't want Jenny to be treated the way I was when I was pregnant with Adam." But, did Adam know about this?

"I really had forgotten about you being pregnant. I guess if anyone would know what it feels like to be pregnant and not married it would be you."

"I'm not proud of it. But I do believe that God allows things to happen to teach us from the experience." I just couldn't help but think about the possibility of being a grandmother.

"Carol, do you think Adam knows?"

"I would say that he does. I think he really loves Jenny. After all, he was on his way home the night of the accident when he turned around to go back after Jenny."

"If he does know, then why hasn't he told me?"

"I can't answer that one."

"You know me. I'll ask the next time I see him. I'll bet he knows and must be happy about Jenny having a baby."

We finished our lunch and Carol drove me back to the office. I thanked her for telling me about Jenny. Now I would have something to look forward to. My first grandchild.

# Chapter 19

On the 5th of January 1984, Adam had a hearing. It started as it always did. "Please rise for the Honorable Judge Bruce C. Embrey. You may be seated." I thought how much more honor and dignity was bestowed upon a judge, say compared to our minister, or any other minister for that matter. I was sure that all of the honor wasn't as pure as the court would have one to believe. I just couldn't get over my feeling. The judge was a rather handsome man with white hair and a neat appearance. He would appear to be a very likeable man under normal circumstances.

Today would be the day the new prosecutor would be there. I wondered if he was as mean as his fellow attorneys thought he would be in his newly acquired position.

"This is Case Number F-33-82S, State of Indiana versus Adam A. Mitchell. Mr. Criss, you're representing Mr. Mitchell and Mr. Spahr, the State of Indiana. We appeared in this Court on the…

"Sixth of December," said Mr. Spahr.

"Sixth of December…the Defendant requested that counsel be appointed. The Court appointed Mr. Criss to represent him. Mr. Criss, have you had the opportunity to consult with Mr. Mitchell during this period of time?"

"I have, but Mr. Mitchell just told me something that would indicate to me I need to talk with him for a couple of minutes."

"All right. We'll take a short recess and let you do that."

Adam hadn't said anything to me. I wondered what he was up to. I watched as Adam and Mr. Criss talked quietly to one another, but I couldn't make out what they were saying.

"Okay. Mr. Criss, are we ready to proceed at this time?"

"Yes, your Honor, we are."

"And, have you now had an opportunity to talk with your client concerning this matter?"

"Yes. I have, Judge. My client intends to deny the allegation that brought him back to court."

"All right. Can we set this final hearing, then, within the next...within the next two weeks? No longer than that."

"Mr. Spahr, how long will it take you to get a witness?"

"However long it takes to get a subpoena up to Fort Wayne and get 'em down here, Judge. I would assume two weeks would get'er done."

"Okay. I'm not sure when this was placed in the file, but Mr. Criss, have you gotten a copy of the report from Washington House?"

"Yes, I have."

"Okay, very good. I think that's the only document that's going to be relevant to the hearing. Okay, Mr. Spahr, if you will get hold of Washington House and find out when you could get your witness here. You might want to call from the Court's phone so we can check the calendar and..."

The Judge didn't finish what he was going to say before Mr. Spahr said, "Very good."

"Let's get this set as quickly as possible," Judge Embrey said.

# **Chapter 20**

January was always cold and depressing for me and I missed the South and the sunshine so much during the winter months that it was hard for me to get up and get moving on such cold mornings. I was still sleeping when the phone rang.

"Hello."

"Hi, it's me. I need you to come and get me. I had a minor surgery this morning and they won't let me drive home," Clay said.

"I'll be there as soon as I get dressed. Where should I pick you up?"

"I'll be just inside at the Out-Patient entrance at St. Joseph Hospital."

"See you in about 30 minutes." I hurried through a shower and dressed quickly. It felt good to know Clay needed me even if it was just to drive him home. I had felt so unneeded by him most of our married life. I had always needed him, and right this particular moment I couldn't recall him needing me, except, of course, for the partner thing as in square dancing, deer hunting, a fishing buddy and carpenter's helper. I wouldn't think about that now. He had asked me to do him a favor and I was going to be smiling when I picked him up.

I pulled up to the entrance of the hospital and before I could get out of the car there was an attendant pushing him out through the double doors.

"I'm glad I caught you before you left for work. I didn't know who else to call," Clay said, somewhat apologetically.

*And Good Morning to you, too!* I thought, but replied with a smile. "I'm glad I could be of some help to you. May I ask what you had to have surgery for?"

"The doctor cleaned out my urethra tube. I'm supposed to take it easy today and then I'll be okay."

"I'm glad it's nothing serious. I have to go to Ft. Wayne today and pick up Adam's things. I'll stop and check on you when I get back."

When we arrived in front of Clay's house he got out and then leaned into the car. "Thanks for coming after me. Maybe when you get back we can go pick up my truck. See you later."

I had to make the trip to Fort Wayne to pick up Adam's personal belongings, and thought I would stop on my way home and talk to the attorney who had been appointed by the court to represent Adam and see if he was going to be a little more understanding of Adam's needs. The drive to Fort Wayne was peaceful and it gave me time to reflect on our pending divorce. I was feeling like I had made a mistake in filing for a divorce from Clay. He was a good man in many ways and I missed him. It was nice to see him at the beginning of my day. I picked up Adam's things in Fort Wayne and drove back to Peru and located the office of Adam's new attorney.

I was lucky. Charles H. Criss was in his office when I arrived.

"Do you have an appointment?" the receptionist asked.

"No, ma'am, but I was wondering if Mr. Criss would have a few minutes to talk to me. I'm Adam Mitchell's mother and Mr. Criss has been appointed to represent my son on a probation violation."

"Just a minute and I'll see."

Annette Bergman

I took a seat and waited for the young girl to return.

"Mr. Criss will see you now."

Attorney Criss greeted me as I walked into his office. After a few pleasantries, I jumped right into the purpose of my visit.

"I appreciate you taking the time to see me. I wanted to explain a few things to you about my son. The court said it was going to get him some help. I don't feel that Adam has had the help he needs. He was in counseling before this accident happened but after they released him from St. Vincent's he hasn't had any follow-up treatment. Adam is a very immature teenager. The court sent him to a halfway house in Marion and you should've seen it. It was filthy and the cook was drunk most of the time. Come to find out the Probation Officer had never set foot in the facility before she sent him over there. He called me one night because a man had broken in and had tried to rape him. I called the Marion Police and was told to get my son out of there, that the place was bad news. The police officer asked me why my son was there and when I told him he said 'I don't care what he's done, get him out of that place.'"

Criss seemed to be paying close attention to my story.

"I was hoping you could get Adam placed where he can get the help he needs to deal with this situation, not put him somewhere that just makes matters worse."

"Mrs. Mitchell, this case has been cut and dried from day one. The judge is going to send him to prison and there is nothing you or I can do about it. We're just going through the motions."

"Is this what you learned in *law school*, just to go with the flow and not make any waves in the system? I can't believe you people. You make up your minds between

170

yourselves and then go through the motions in court. The facts or circumstances have nothing to do with it. I'm still upset that a Marion County Sheriff's Deputy *hit and killed* two teenagers and they *forgot* to do a blood alcohol test and when they remembered the *next* morning his alcohol content was .16. Those two kids aren't any less dead than that State Trooper. My son got *five years* and Sergeant Atwell gets 6 months *probation.* The Mothers Against Drunk Drivers think they had a victory. I have news for you people. A victory is equal justice and this is not even close."

Mr. Criss seemed somewhere between shocked and scolded.

"I'll do what I can, but I can't make any promises." His face was red and he looked embarrassed, like a child who had been caught with his hand in the cookie jar.

"That's all I ask. Just don't be a puppet on a string. There are enough attorneys that are puppets. All I ask is that you try. Adam was in counseling when this accident happened and no one wanted to look at the problems he was having. Adam should be helped, not treated like a common criminal. I appreciate you listening to me. Thank you."

I left without another word, my heart pounding. It seemed to me that anger fueled my strength to go on. I drove the 15 miles back to Kokomo with my mind in a whirlwind, thinking if there was a way to scrutinize the judges who took part in some of the privilege cases and disbarred them, a lot of the cases would come out differently.

"I can't take on the judicial system in Indiana," I told myself. "I need to concentrate on helping Adam get through this and find out about Jenny and when the baby is due."

*Annette Bergman*

It was late afternoon when I got back to my office.
Almost thankful that no one was looking for me, I called
Clay. The phone rang and rang. No answer, I tried several
more times and decided I should drive over there. I
knocked at the door. "Come in," came a weak voice. Clay
was on the couch, there was vomit on the floor. I felt his
head. "You're burning up with fever. What's wrong?"

"I don't know. The doctor gave me a prescription, but I
didn't have it filled yet."

"Tell me where it is and I'll go and get it filled. Do you
want me to call the doctor?'

"No, just get the prescription filled and maybe I'll get to
feeling better."

When I returned I first gave Clay his medicine and then
started cleaning up the vomit from the floor.

Clay asked, "Could you help me to the bathroom?"

He was weak. I had never seen Clay that sick before. I
helped him into the bathroom.

"I'll wait at the door. You call me when you're through
and I'll help you. Don't try to move around by yourself."

When he called for me to help him I couldn't help
noticing the blood. "Clay, should you be bleeding like
this?"

"I don't think so. Maybe you should call the doctor."

I helped him to the bed and then went to the living room
to call the doctor. The doctor told me to keep him off of his
feet and to keep taking the medicine and it should clear up.
An infection had probably set in because he hadn't started
on the medicine soon enough. I went to tell Clay, but he
was asleep. I went back into the living room to finish
cleaning some spots on the couch.

I noticed some pictures on an end table at the end of the sofa. I picked them up and saw that they were pictures that Clay had taken when we went on our last deer hunting trip together. It was after the divorce and we were both in a state of uncertainty. We had always loved going hunting together and I remembered the heartache that I felt because my stubborn pride wouldn't let me tell Clay how much I really loved him. There had been times that we were both thinking the same thing and were so comfortable together. Clay had always been willing to help me do physical things and I had always been there for him. Now, Clay just couldn't provide me with the affection and support that I so desperately needed.

Clay and I never went anywhere but square dancing, camping and deer hunting - all the things Clay enjoyed.

I found a pen and made some notes on the back of the pictures.

The phone rang and I rushed to answer it.

"Hello."

"Well...is Clay there?"

It was a woman's voice and I wondered who it could be.

"No...yes he is here...but he can't come to the phone. Could I take a message?"

"Well..." it seemed the woman didn't want to be identified.

"You could leave a number and I'll have him call."

"WELL...!"

The sound of her voice made me think that she was upset that I had answered the phone. The silence and lack of conversation launched the reply.

"Look lady...his stud service is closed. Try back in about a month or so."

"Well...I *never*."

I hung up the phone. Now certain that Clay really did have someone else in his life, I picked up the pictures again and wrote intimate things that never happened on the back of the pictures. I carefully stacked the pictures and returned them to their folder, thinking that one day his new friend would see them. I secretly hoped whoever it was would be jealous of me.

After lunch the next day Clay said. "You can go home now. I feel much better."

"I'll stay longer if you think you need me."

"No, I'll be fine. Thanks for helping me out."

I liked being there for him and hated it when he told me he didn't need me to help him anymore.

# Chapter 21

I returned home late in the afternoon of January 9$^{th}$ 1984 to find a stack of mail. I was sorting through the mail when the phone rang.

"Hello."

"Hi. It's Jenny. I'm in the hospital. I have some good news and I have some bad news. The good news is, I had the baby and it was a boy. I named him Wesley after my father. The bad news...he died. She was crying and I couldn't believe my ears. I wanted to know what had happened but Jenny was much too upset to be telling me the details on the telephone.

"Jenny, which hospital are you in?"

"St. Joseph's...room 212."

"I'll be right there."

I raced out of the house and across town to the hospital. My mind was in a whirl as I drove into the hospital parking area. "I hate this parking lot. You can tell some man designed it. You have to drive around in circles to get to the parking area," I said out loud. It seemed to be miles across the lot and then you had to walk down such long corridors to the patients' rooms.

I entered the room and Jenny was facing away from me. I called her name softly in case she was sleeping. Jenny turned toward me, wiping the tears away as she rolled over. I leaned over the bed and gave her a long and silent hug. We were both crying now and clinging to one another for dear life. It was obvious to me that Jenny hadn't had enough hugging and she was in deep grief over the loss of her baby.

Jenny had seen her father killed when she was a child, and had been thrown out of the house by her parents as a teenager. This was more than any seventeen-year-old needed. She had gone through enough grief to last a lifetime. Now she would have to accept the loss of her first born child.

"Jenny, what caused the baby to die?"

"They said he had an enlarged heart and that his lungs weren't developed."

"This just doesn't seem fair. I just found out that you were pregnant and now here you are going through a terrible time all by yourself."

"My mom came up."

"That's good, Jenny. Did Adam know you were pregnant?"

"Yes," she answered with her head slightly bowed.

"Jenny, why didn't the two of you tell me?"

"We didn't want you to worry. You had the lawsuits to deal with and trying to work and your mother to worry about. We didn't think you needed anything else to worry about."

"Oh, Jenny, I would have seen this as a gift from God. It would have been a bright spot in these troubled times. Where are you staying now?"

"I'm living with an older couple. I help take care of his wife because she had a stroke."

"I thought you were living with your grandmother?"

"Naw, she kicked me out when she found out I was pregnant."

Poor Jenny, she had been living with almost strangers because her parents had rejected her and even her once-loving and devoted grandmother wouldn't let her live with her because she was pregnant and not married.

"Jenny, we don't know why these things happen, but they do, and all we can do is ask God for strength to get us through them. I want you to remember that there is a purpose for this. We don't know what it is now, but one day we will understand it better. Is there anything I can do for you?"

"Yes, please tell Adam."

"I was wondering if you had tried to notify him." She shook her head as the tears continued to flow. What grief was on the face on this young mother, so thin and pale, with her long blonde hair tossed and uncombed.

"I'll call Adam's probation officer and see if I can go to Peru and tell him in person. I don't want to tell him on the phone."

"Okay," she said.

Jenny looked exhausted. "You need to get some rest, I'll see you tomorrow."


The next morning I called Adam's probation officer and explained the situation and she gave me permission for me to see my son and give him the news about his and Jenny' baby.

They had a special room where you could spend time with an inmate as long as there was a guard present. I waited for them to bring my son in. Adam took one look at me and knew something was terrible wrong.

"What's happened?"

I gave Adam a hug and while still standing face to face with him and said.

"Jenny had the baby...and it was a little boy." I started to cry.

"He died."

His knees went weak and I had to hold him up. It was like the final blow to his endurance. The news about the baby was more than he could take. Adam broke down and cried for sometime before he could get himself under control. I looked at the guard and I could tell that his heart went out to both of us.

After he gained some composure Adam asked, "How's Jenny taking this?"

"Believe it or not she seems to be doing well under the circumstances. It was late afternoon yesterday when she called me and I went to the hospital right away. I could tell she had been crying, but then who wouldn't cry at a time like this?"

"When is the funeral? Mom, do you think they will let me see the baby?"

"Adam, I'll do everything in my power to get you to Kokomo to see the baby. I'm sure Jenny would like to see you, too. I can only stay for a few minutes now. I just couldn't tell you about this over the phone. Adam, you have to believe that God knows best and we have to keep our faith in God. I'll call Diana as soon as I know about the funeral arrangements and see if she can get you to the funeral home. I love you very much and I know that this hurts more than words can say, but we will live through this and I promise you there will be brighter days."

I turned to go, then I turned back.

"Adam, why didn't you tell me about the baby?"

"Mom, I've caused you so much heartache. I just couldn't tell you about this."

"It's okay, Adam. I just wish you felt more like talking to me. I'm your mother and I'll always love you no matter what. You and Jenny aren't the first young couple to get into trouble and you won't be the last."

"I should have known you'd understand."

"Honey, I have to go. I need to find out about the funeral and see if Diane can make arrangements for you to be there. Take care of yourself and remember that God doesn't give us more than we can handle."

"Are you sure?"

"Yes, honey I am. We're just being tested. I'll see you soon. I love you, Adam."

"I love you, too, Mom."

I gave my son another hug and was shown out of the room. I didn't even make it to the car before I started wiping away tears. It was so difficult for me to try to keep Adam's spirits up when my own were as low as his. I sat in the car crying until I could see to drive back home.


The funeral arrangements for little Wesley were made and the probation officer had made arrangements for Adam to come to the funeral parlor to see his son.

The tiny body lay in a small coffin and the baby was dressed in an aqua colored sleeper. He looked so peaceful, I just wanted to pick him up and hold him in my arms. He looked like he was sleeping. His soft blond hair wasn't much more than fuzz and he looked like Adam had as a baby.

I heard the door to the funeral parlor open and the winter winds rushing in. I looked up and Adam was brought in with handcuffs. The sheriff removed the cuffs and Adam walked straight over to where the baby lay. Jenny spotted him and almost ran to be by his side. The two tall thin figures embraced and started weeping in each other's arms. An officer finally gave Adam a nudge so he could lead him to the back of the funeral parlor. I joined him there and tried to console him. Adam and Jenny sat at the back of the room talking quietly. Jenny still had her coat on, and it looked two sizes too big for her. What a heart breaking sight the two of them were. The officer informed Adam that his time was up. He had only been allowed to see the baby for that short period of time and now he had to leave. It wasn't what I had hoped for, but it was better than Adam never getting to see his son.

I followed him as the officer led Adam to the entrance of the funeral home.

"Adam, I'll be there on Sunday," I said to him as the door was closing. The service was short and the drive to the grave was slow. There was fresh snow on the ground and the winter winds were blowing as they laid little Wesley to rest on January 12, 1984. I stood at the grave in my beige trench coat with a white fur hat, looking stylish, but feeling like my heart was breaking. I looked upward to the sky and said, "God, if I can live through this, I can live through anything, This is definitely one of the saddest days of my life."

I watched as they lowered the tiny casket into the ground, wondering what little Wesley would have been like had he been given a chance to live. Would he have grown up to have red hair, big blue eyes and freckles like his daddy? We'd never know.

# **Chapter 22**

It had been a week since the baby's funeral and the sheriff had called to say that Adam wasn't eating and wondered if I would come to the jail to see him and try to get him to snap out of his depression. He told me if something wasn't done that they were going to have to put Adam in the hospital. I assured the Sheriff that I would be there the next day for a special visit with Adam. I called Jenny and asked if she would like to go with me.

I thought that maybe Jenny could bring him out of his depression faster than I could. If he could see Jenny, and see how well she was doing then maybe Adam could get his mind on Jenny and off the loss of the baby.

I picked Jenny up at the home of the couple whom she was staying with and the two of us drove toward Peru.

"How're things going for you, Jenny?" I asked.

"I'm okay. I'm really glad that you called. I've wanted to see Adam and I didn't know if they would let me."

"I'm not sure that they are going to let you, Jenny, but I thought this would be a good time to take you there and find out. They called last night and asked me to come and talk to him because he isn't eating, and they said he's really depressed. I thought that you could bring him out of his depression faster than anyone else."

The sheriff agreed to let Jenny see Adam, and we were let into the private room where Adam sat waiting.

"Hi, Jenny," Adam said in a soft voice. "How ya doing?" I could see Adam was surprised to see her.

"We're not here about me. What's this I hear about you not eating?"

"I haven't been hungry."

"Your Mom said they're going to put you in the hospital if you don't start eating.  You're so thin anyway you can't afford not to eat." Jenny almost glowed when she talked to Adam.

It was obvious that the two of them had a special love for one another, and I was glad Adam had a chance to see Jenny.

I asked the guard if I could be excused so the two of them could have some time together. I sat in the waiting room replaying in my mind the awful turn of events since Adam's accident. My mother's stroke, Clay's withdrawal, finding out Jenny was pregnant and thinking that would be the joy that would be there for Adam to look forward to, and then the death of the baby.  I wondered how much an nineteen-year old could endure.

It wasn't long until Jenny opened the door to come out that I was allowed a few seconds to put my arms around my son. I could feel his bones as I hugged him.  He was too thin now. He had never been a heavy person, but now he was thinner than ever.

"Adam, please eat.  I can't go on without you," I whispered in his ear.

"I'll eat, Mom. Please don't worry about me. I promise I'll eat."

Jenny and I left and were feeling better that we had gotten to see Adam.

Several days later this letter arrived:

*Dear Mom,*

*It's 3:00 in the morning and I can't sleep. I'm glad they let me go to the baby's funeral. I'm doing a little better. I still can't believe it. It all seems so unreal. I wish I would wake up in the morning and discover it was all a bad dream.*

*I'm not much when it comes to things like this. I know I'm not doing myself any good thinking about it all the time. I have to let it all out anyway that I can because keeping it in will make it hurt longer. Like the other things that I have kept inside. All it did was prolong the pain. I can't do that to myself again.*

*I can't let it eat away at me like before. I trust God will let some good come of this. I'm not happy about the whole thing, but God's will be done, not mine. At least I know that Wesley is in heaven, and I pray that God will be merciful, and grant him eternal life. He is in a far better place than we are. I know I hurt because I'm selfish and God wants us to rejoice in death I feel better having written to you. I'm looking forward to seeing you this weekend.*

Love Always,
Adam

A few weeks passed and Jenny called me on a Sunday afternoon.

"Paige."

"What is it, Jenny?"

"The man whose house I'm staying at tried to make me have sex with him. He said I had sex with Adam and I should have sex with him, because his wife had a stroke and she can't have sex with him anymore."

"Pack your things, Jenny, I'm on my way to pick you up. You can live here with me. I'll be right there."

I grabbed my purse and keys and hurried to my car. It was several miles to where Jenny was staying and I had time to think about Jenny living with me. I liked the idea. I thought maybe the two of us could be of help to one another. Jenny wasn't in sight when I pulled into the stone driveway of the country home. It looked slightly rundown, with its peeling paint and clutter sitting on the open porch. I honked the horn. Jenny appeared at the door with a small suitcase and a few things under her arm. I felt sorry for her immediately. She too was thin and her face was drawn and pale. *This isn't how life is supposed to be for young people,* I thought. Jenny opened the back door of the car and put her things in. Another phase of her life was just beginning. Jenny and I headed home together.

It was good to have Jenny in the house. I put her in the bedroom upstairs across from Adam's room. We would sit up at night and talk about different things and I was glad that Jenny was living in my home. I was getting to know Jenny better and felt like she was mature beyond her 18 years.

We sat in the living room, each feeling better that the other one was there.

"Jenny, have you ever thought about going to school and learning a trade?"

"Not really. I've been told that I'm a slow learner and I probably can't learn a trade," she answered.

"Being slow doesn't mean you can't learn. Everybody has a gift to do something. Some people go through life without ever finding out what their gift is. If you like to do something, chances are that you'll be good at it. I liked being a beautician when I worked at it. The ladies usually left the shop feeling better and looking better, and it made me feel good to make them look better. You are so easy to talk to, and that goes along way with being a good beautician."

"I always wanted to go to beauty school. I have social security benefits because of my Dad being dead. I think they would pay for it."

"That's great, Jenny. We'll go to the beauty school first thing in the morning and get you enrolled. I know the owner. His name is Martin. You'll like him."

I took Jenny to the Wright's Beauty College the next morning and enrolled her for school. We were both excited about the possibilities for Jenny's new career. We left there and went to a department store.

"What are we stopping here for?" Jenny asked.

"We're going to buy you some uniforms to start school in."

"Paige you can't spend money on me."

"I can, too. I work for my money and I can spend it anyway I want to. I'd like to think that this is an opportunity for you, Jenny, and I want you to have what you need to feel good about yourself and do well in school. Not only that, I want to prove to the person or persons that said you were slow that they don't know what they are talking about. Someone once said that you could feed a man a fish for a day or you can teach him to fish and he can feed himself for a lifetime. We're teaching you how to fish, and in this case you need a couple of white uniforms and a good pair of shoes."

We were in the uniform department by then and the two of us were looking at this new adventure with the same view. Jenny found two uniforms that she liked, so I paid for them. She was smiling and seemed happy. We moved on to the shoe department.

"You're spending too much money on me," Jenny protested.

I wasn't concerned about the small investment I was making in Jenny. "Look, Jenny, you need this and I need it for you. I tell you what, someday, when you have the opportunity to help someone have a better life you can pass it on and we'll be even. How's that?"

She just smiled and made a slight nod with her head. She had the sweetest and kindest look about her and I was sure that this was, indeed, going to change Jenny's life.

Adam was due back in court on the second of February for a probation violation.

# Chapter 23

The wind was howling and the temperature was close to zero when I exited the car to put money in the parking meter in front of the courthouse in Peru. I again climbed the white marble stairs to the third floor looking out of the huge windows on the landing between the floors. The brick paved street to the north of the courthouse had few cars parked in the normally full parking spaces. I opened the tall doors and entered the Miami Superior Courtroom. People were chatting among themselves if they had someone next to them to talk with. I always had that sick feeling in my stomach that I just couldn't seem to control. I took a seat as close to the defense table as I could get. Adam was already there with his attorney. He turned and smiled at me.

The bailiff stood and said, "Be it remembered, on the 2nd day of February 1984, the same being Calendar Year 1984, the above and foregoing cause of action came to be heard before the Honorable Bruce C. Embrey, sole Judge of the Miami Superior Court. All rise."

"This is Cause Number F-33-82S, State of Indiana verses Adam A. Mitchell. Mr. Criss, you're representing Mr. Mitchell; Mr. Spahr, the State of Indiana. We're here on a probation revocation hearing today. Mr. Criss, is it your intent to put the State to the burden of proving the violation?"

"It is."

"All right. The Court received from Mr. Mitchell, and I think a copy was forwarded to both of you, a letter which is without date on the letter itself. It was written in January, and I can't make out the date on it. Did each of you receive a copy of that?"

Both attorneys answered yes.

"Are we ready to proceed?"

"The State is. May it please the Court and counsel, the evidence the State will introduce will show that, on or about November the 28th, 1983, the defendant, Adam Mitchell, was living or residing at the 13 Step House in Fort Wayne and that he was observed in the facility, appeared to be intoxicated by a resident there, Mr. Thompson. That following that observation, Mr. Thompson reported that fact to Jack Khan. Mr. Khan came up, observed the defendant vomiting and gaffing in the bathroom, smelling of alcohol. Mr. Kahn confronted him. The defendant denied at first and then later there was an admission that he had been drinking. He took the gentleman from the 13 Step House as is required under the rules of the house, to the Washington House, which is a detox center in Fort Wayne, approximately a mile distant. Washington House evaluated him. He basically passed out there, vomited there, passed out, had to be undressed, put into pajamas, and was retained at the detox center until he was released to the authorities. Everybody who observed his conduct has evaluated and believes that the defendant had been drinking. A beer can was found in his pocket at the detox center, and with that evidence we believe the State will be able to show by a preponderance of the evidence that the defendant has violated the terms of his probation, specifically rule number seven. Thank you, Judge."

"Okay, Mr. Criss."

"Your Honor, Mr. Mitchell will rest on his right to require the State to prove its case."

"Call Diane Monaghan."

"Diane Monaghan, do you swear to tell the truth, the whole truth, and nothing but the truth?"

"I do."

"State you name and occupation, please."

"Diane Monaghan, probation officer."

"Are you acquainted with the defendant, Adam Mitchell?"

"Yes, I am."

"And, if you would, give me some idea of how Mr. Mitchell came to be at 13 Step House in Fort Wayne."

"He was, um, Adam had gone through…was diagnosed by the department of mental health as an alcohol abuser, and it was recommended that he enter Richmond State Hospital for that alcohol program. Adam went to the Central State Hospital and completed the program there, which I believe to be about 49 days. He was returned to the Miami County Jail, and we secured placement for him at the 13th Step House in Fort Wayne."

"Is there any connection with the proceeding leading up to his placement at the 13th Step House in Fort Wayne? Did this Court enter an order on October 27, 1983, setting out specific terms of probation while at that residence?"

"Yes."

"And, specifically, item seven under that order, do you recall what it provided for?"

"I believe that part of the order indicated that Adam was not allowed to possess or consume alcohol or drugs while there."

"Illegal drugs or controlled substances while at that residence?"

"While at the 13th Step House."

"All right. Here now is a copy of that order given to Mitchell?"

"Yes, it was."

"And who gave it to him?"

"I believe probably Dan Doyle from our office. Dan transported Adam to the 13th Step House, and I believe he was armed with an order."

"All right, and was a copy of the order furnished to 13th Step House as well?"

"Yes, it was."

"Did you initiate and file a Petition to Modify or Revoke Probation with regard to the defendant?"

"Yes."

"And was that filed on November 29 of '83?"

"Yes, it was."

"And it recited that there has been a violation, I believe, of Rule 7, in that on November 28th of 1983, Adam Mitchell consumed an alcoholic beverage while at the 13th Step House, is that correct?"

"That's correct."

"You have no personal knowledge of that actual alcohol consumption yourself though, do you?"

"No, I do not."

"Okay, who furnished you that information?"

"Uh, Dan Doyle from our alcohol program in the office, indicated that he received…"

"Objection, your Honor, hearsay."

Well now, Diana Monaghan can't testify to what someone else said, but Trooper Roland can testify to what Mr. Wink said he saw during the accident. I don't understand. It just seems to me that we are still just going through what was *cut and dried* from the beginning according to Mr. Criss.

"You had received information from some other source?"

"Objection, your Honor, leading question," protested Mr. Criss.

"She may respond to that," the Judge interjected.

"Yes, I received it from a different source."

"Nothing further from this witness."

"Mr. Criss," the Judge said.

"Miss Monaghan, you haven't given any recommendations to the Court as far as I'm aware. Is that correct."

"No, I have not."

"Have you had a chance to evaluate all the findings that you've received and are you in file regarding this hearing?"

"Yes."

"What's your recommendation, if you have any?"

"I feel that Adam should be committed to the Department of Corrections."

I wondered if that was truly Diane's recommendation, or if this case had in fact caused her too many migraines, as she had stated earlier at our home.

"Can you tell the Court why you feel that way?"

"I feel that the Court and the community have exhausted all resources for Adam."

What had the community done for Adam other than have a reporter from the Peru Daily newspaper try to influence the Judge not to take his plea agreement, because he didn't have the guts to write about the *other plea agreements that had come for the third floor of the courthouse*, as he testified in court.

"What are those available to the community?"

"Um, halfway houses for alcohol treatment, um…"

"Let me go back. What do you think Adam's main problem is?"

"I feel Adam has a good deal of emotional problems, but that he compounds these problems through the use of alcohol and drugs."

"Would you say that he's an alcoholic?"

"In the time that I've known Adam, I would have to say yes."

"Was the original conduct which brought Mr. Mitchell to your attention combined with the use of alcohol?"

"Yes."

"All right, now what are these resources available in the community for this alcoholism that had been expended for him?"

"We placed Adam at the Genesis House in Marion, Indiana. He did not successfully…"

"Well now, what is the Genesis House?"

"It's a halfway house for alcohol users."

"Was that the first placement for Adam?"

"Yes, it was"

"All right, when would that have been?"

"I believe Adam went in January of '83."

"All right, he was sentenced back in when?"

"November of '82."

"All right, what happened between those times?"

"He remained in jail."

"Okay. Now, you said the Genesis House is a halfway house?"

"Yes."

"All right, Halfway house for?"

"Alcohol users."

"All right, how was his progress there?"

"I would indicate poor."

"Could you tell us why?"

"I think it was lack of motivation on Adam's part, and some shortcoming of the Genesis House and staff."

"Why was the decision made at that time, then, to place him in a halfway house and not some other program?"

"Pardon me?"

"Why was the decision made, or how was the decision made to place him in a halfway house, rather than some other program?"

"We just felt that with what goals Adam had and what he needed to achieve could be properly done in a halfway house."

"I don't believe Richmond State Hospital would take him at the time, either," interjected the Judge.

"I don't recall."

"It's your opinion, however, that that program failed or Adam failed the program, or it failed him?"

"A combination of the two, yes."

"All right, then what occurred as far as placement?"

"He was returned from the Genesis House and placed in the Miami County Jail, at which time we asked the Department of Mental Health to evaluate him for treatment as an alcohol abuser within the State system. The department indicated that it felt he did meet its criteria and recommended that he be placed at Central State Hospital for its program."

"All right, he was subsequently placed there, was he not?"

"Yes."

"What was the outcome of that placement?"

"He satisfactorily completed the program."

"All right, he satisfactorily completed the program. What was your recommendation?"

"My recommendation was that he go to the halfway house."

"And then what happened?"

"He was transported from Central State Hospital to the Miami County Jail to await contact with the 13th Step House to see if they would accept him."

"Was that his ultimate placement next?"

"Yes."

"All right, you're testifying here with information you received he failed at the 13th Step House?"

"Yes."

"Okay. During any of these placements on behalf of Adam, was the Richmond State Program considered as a possible alternative?"

"It was considered by me. In fact, that's why I thought the Department of Mental health would place him there, but they indicated that they felt Central State's program suited his needs."

"Now, what is the difference in the two programs, between Central State and Richmond State?"

"Central State Hospital is a 49-day program based, on and geared toward individualized counseling. Richmond State is a six-month program that is geared toward group therapy, and everything…all dealings with Adam are completed by a group there. He does not have individual counseling at Richmond. They felt with Adam's problems, compounded by his drinking, his use of alcohol, that individualized program would suit him better than the group."

"Now, am I correct in assuming that Richmond State is likewise a drug treatment facility?"

"Yes, it is."

"As well as alcohol?"

"Yes."

"Okay. Would you make a recommendation to the Court to have Adam placed in Richmond State Hospital for alcohol counseling?"

"Would I? No, that's not possible."

"All right, why is that not possible? Why would you make that recommendation?"

"Richmond State Hospital is not in our catchment area, so in order to have someone placed in a facility outside of our catchment area, the Department of Mental Health would have to become involved and may demand that they designate the place of treatment, if we choose to go outside of our catchment area."

"You say it's not possible, I'm still not clear on why it's not possible."

"Because DAS saw that it was not feasible at the time that we requested placement of Adam originally within a state facility."

"I understand that, but why is it not possible now?"

"Because I don't think the Department of Mental Health has made their finding on Adam. If they had thought that it was appropriate that he go to Richmond, they would have placed him there. I don't see any finding now that are any different that would make a difference."

"Have you checked with the Department of Mental Health as to whether it's possible now or not?"

"No, I have not."

"Okay. Then what you're talking to us about now is your opinion."

"Yes, that's my opinion."

"Okay, no further questions, your Honor."

"You may step down," the Judge said.

"Call Robert Thompson," said Mr. Spahr.

"Do you swear to tell the truth, the whole truth, and nothing but the truth?"

"I do."

"State your name, please."

"Robert Thompson."

"Mr. Thompson, where do you reside?"

"13th Step House, Fort Wayne."

"Okay, that's 1317 West Washington Street?"

"Yes, sir."

"And how long have you been a resident there?"

"Fourteen months."

"All right, I turn your attention to November the 28th, 1983. Do you recall that date and where you were at the time?"

"Yes, I was on duty then."

"All right, do you recall observing Adam Mitchell, the defendant in this matter, in 13th Step House on that date?"

"Yes."

"All right, why don't you relate to the Court what you observed occurring that evening involving the defendant Adam Mitchell?"

"Well, I set at the desk in the office and he came in, and he started to get ready to go up the stairs, and he was actin' different than what he usually does. I followed him upstairs and he was in the bathroom with the basin runnin' and he was throwin' up and gagging. I waited until he came out and asked him if he had been drinking. He said no, but I smelled it on his breath. I told him I thought he had, and I went downstairs and called the manager."

"Who is the manager?"

"Jack Khan."

"Well, what happened after that?"

"Well, he came over and he took over after that."

"All right, did you leave the defendant then and make that call?"

"I had to, he was upstairs. The only phone we have is downstairs."

"All right. Other than smelling alcoholic beverages on his breath and vomiting, was there any other indication to you that he had been drinking?"

"No."

"Okay, you didn't see any cans on him?"

"No."

"Okay. Do you remember what he might have been wearing at that time?"

"I don't have the slightest idea."

"No other questions," said Spahr.

"What time of the evening was this, do you recall?" asked the Judge.

"Well, I don't know for sure. It was after dark."

"Judge, I think I can clarify the time better a little later. No other questions."

"Mr. Criss." The Judge called for his cross-examination.

"Mr. Thompson, is there anything in your experience that would cause alcohol breath other than alcohol?"

"No. See, I'm an alcoholic. I don't know anything but alcohol. I've never had drugs or anything."

"Have you ever had any opportunity to drink alcohol?"

"Have I?"

"Yes."

"Oh, yes."

"Well, have you had an opportunity to also chew on a breath mint or something like that?"

"Yeah."

"Okay, now, if I'm understanding, you said Mr. Mitchell said he was not drinking that night."

"Yes."

"Have you ever had an opportunity in past experiences with food poisoning or something that might cause you to throw up?"

"No. I've been sick to my stomach and threw up."

"And you've thrown up because you were sick to your stomach"

"Uh-huh."

"I see."

"No further questions."

"You can step down, Mr. Thompson, thank you," said Judge Embrey.

"Call Jack Khan," said Spahr.

Jack Kahn, was sworn in.

"State your name and occupation, please."

"Jack Khan, manager of 13th Step House, Fort Wayne, Indiana."

"All right, and how long have you been employed as manager there?"

"Almost eleven years."

"Were you acquainted, are you acquainted with Adam Mitchell?"

"Yes, very much."

"In what capacity?"

"He became a friend after moving into the 13th Step House, and I remember the order you spoke of, the rules that he was to have gone by. He went by them for 28 days. And he was in every night. He went to AA meetings regularly. He got some part time work, not a lot, but he got some work. And went by our rules just fine until that one night."

"Which night are you talking about?"

"It would have been November the 28th. It was approximately...the call came at approximately, I guess, around ten minutes till eleven. I'd just gone home a couple hours prior to that. It was around ten minutes to eleven."

"Okay, so you received a call from somebody. Who was that that called?"

"Robert Thompson."

"Right, and what did Mr. Thompson tell you?"

"He told me that Adam was acting pretty strange. He was upstairs and that I better get over there right away."

"And what did you do in response to the call?"

"I came right over to the 13th Step House and went upstairs. Adam was in the bathroom again. I was told he was in there before, he was in there at that time, and I did hear him vomiting. I finally got him to open the door and I said, 'Adam have you been drinking?' He denied that at first and then he said that he had a couple. He also indicated that he wanted to stay that night and go to work tomorrow, but our rules at Step House, you just cannot do that. However, we did find a can of malt liquor in the dresser drawer there. I got him over to the bed, and said, 'Adam, you can't stay here. It's part of the rules at the Step

House.' I'd like to make…can I make a little statement for me?"

"Let's just wait. Let's finish the testimony. After you got him back into his room, did he complain to you at all about having bad food or being sick from eating bad food?"

"No, he did not."

"Did he smell of any alcoholic beverage?"

"Yes, sir."

"All right. You indicated you found a beer can?"

"In his top dresser drawer."

"Okay."

"One of the large cans of beer."

"What kind of beer is it? Do you recall what it was?"

"It was a Bach beer. It's been a long time since I've drunk."

"It was a can of beer, not a bottle of beer?"

"It was a can, an aluminum can."

"Does he share his room with someone else?"

"With two other individuals."

"Okay. Do they keep their clothes in separate dressers?"

"Separate drawers, right."

"And you indicated you found this can of beer in Adam's dresser?"

"Yes."

"After that, did you transport Adam anywhere?"

"Yes, we took him to the Washington House. I told him he'd have to get dressed and that he'd go to the Washington House. I was open and told him at that time, and meant it, that I would be willing, you know, to bring him back in if the Court allowed, to the 13th Step House and was hoping that would have been possible."

"Is that still the case?"

"That's still the case today."

"Okay. Did you personally transport him to the Washington House?"

"Yes, I went along."

"And to whom did you transport him, once you arrived at the Washington House?"

"A lady named Betsy and Rocky, who are there today"

"Rocky?"

"Well, that's maybe a nickname."

"John Rabar?"

"No."

"No? Excuse me, Reverend Borman?"

"Okay."

"Mr. Borman? You know him as Rocky?"

"I just know him as Rocky."

"Okay, and did you remain around then to watch what happened after that, or…"

"Well, you really kind of have to. He was sitting down. Betsy was taking what information she could get, which was not much, 'cause he passed out at the desk. And then we had to carry him back to the bed that they had for him. And he had vomited in the wastebasket, and of course the smell of alcohol was so prevalent."

"Okay, nothing further."

Mr. Criss stood to start his questioning.

"This can that you found in the dresser drawer, was this empty or was it full?"

"It was a full can."

"A full can. Did you find any empty cans in the room?"

"No, we did not. He came in and went right upstairs."

"Did you conduct any chemical tests on the blood…breath?"

"No, we do not do that there, no."

"You say you've been a manager for how long down there?"

"Almost, it will be eleven years in May."

"Does your 13th Step House treat other people, other than drug and alcohol addicts?"

"It's drug and alcohol, that's all."

"All right. Do you have a mixture between the two?"

"Well, one of the requirements is that they have a problem with alcohol because it was started as a halfway house for alcohol. And we try to kinda stick to that, but like me, I had both problems when I came there, several years ago. That's what I understand."

"You say you're the manager. Have you had any training as far as…in these areas?"

"No, just working with other alcoholics and…I'm not a professional person."

"Okay, do you know if there's anything like a mouthwash or candy or a flavoring agent or something that can smell like alcohol and not be alcohol?"

"I'm sure they exist."

"No further questions"

Mr. Spahr stood and asked. "Did you communicate the events you've testified to any person here in this courthouse after the incident?"

"Ye, I did. I called Dan Doyle. It was a few minutes after midnight, maybe, about five minutes after midnight, and reported to him what had happened. I was gonna kinda wait until the next morning, but I could not go to sleep until I had done that. I called him at home."

"Do you recognize the Adam Mitchell that was a resident of 13th Step House in court today?"

"Yes."

"Where is he seated?"

"Right next, the red headed boy there."

"Okay."

"Let the records show the witness identified the defendant," said the Judge.

"And this is one and the same individual you transported to Washington House?"

"Yes, it is."

"On November 28th?"

"Yes."

"Nothing further," said Spahr.

Mr. Criss getting up from his chair and buttoning his suit coat asked, "You say that the first 27 or 28 days you had no problems as far as Mr. Mitchell breaking your rules?"

"No. He did excellent. I have to say that in all honesty."

"Did you ever find out what caused his conduct that evening?"

"No, you just really never know why one does it. I don't know what caused it. However...I don't know."

"You never had any conversation with him after that then?"

"I talked to him on the phone a couple of times. I thought I would be able to go out and see him, but he was gone before I got the chance. I thought he'd be out there five days, but that wasn't the case."

"No further questions."

"Judge, I have another question. I think it was addressed differently in this last series of questions by counsel. Were any other individuals drinking with the defendant, that you learned about later," asked Mr. Spahr.

"There was, according to what I was told."

Mr. Spahr sat back in his chair and Mr. Criss asked, "How did you learn this information to which you were about to testify?"

"I don't know what you mean"

"Did somebody tell you about what you're to testify to?"

"Yes."

"Are they present in the courtroom today?"

"They are not."

"Objection, your Honor, it's hearsay."

"Sustained."

"Nothing further," stated Spahr.

"You may step down."

Again Mr. Spahr stood. "Call Mr. Borman."

Mr. Borman took his oath.

"State your name, please."

"Herman Borman."

"Do you go by a nickname?"

"Yeah I do, Rocky."

"Okay. And where do you live?"

"I live at 1019 Nelson Street, Fort Wayne, Indiana."

"Are you employed?"

"Yes, I am."

"By whom?"

"The Washington House, Incorporated."

"All right, in what capacity do you work there?"

"I'm a third shift technician."

"Okay, what do you do there?"

"Uh, it's mainly intake, making sure the place doesn't burn down, running vitals all night. It primarily runs into intake."

"When does your shift begin?"

"Eleven o'clock."

"When does it end?"

"Seven."

"Seven in the morning?"

"That's right. We usually relieve...I relieve the second shift at usually twenty-five minutes till eleven, so we relieve early."

"Okay, a little overlap?"

"Right."

"Are you acquainted with Adam Mitchell?"

"Uh, not until the 28th of November, he came in. He was brought in by Jack Khan."

"All right. And do you recognize the Adam Mitchell that was brought in by Jack Khan as being one and the same person that's seated in this courtroom?"

"Yes, I do."

"Why don't you relate to the Court your observations of Adam Mitchell on November the 28th, 1983?"

"Well, Jack and another resident at the Step House brought him in. We have a desk that one person sits on one side and takes the information that we put on our 24-hour charts and the other person stands on the other side to run the initial blood pressure and pulse and to get them into pajamas. You know, take care of anything else along those lines. Adam sat down in the chair that we have people sit in when they check in, and because we do run initial vitals, I had him take his coat off. He sat down, looked like he was gonna get sick, or said he was going to get sick. We got a trash can from behind the desk, brought it over. He got sick, and then he was out."

"By out you mean...?"

"I mean he passed out."

"Okay, unconscious?"

"Unconscious. We…only twice since I've worked at the Washington house have I had to actually take somebody's clothes off, then put him in pajamas, and Adam was the first time."

"Did you find anything, or was there anything on his clothes, in the course of undressing?"

"When I had him take his coat off, and I believe it's the coat he's wearing right now, in fact, there was a weight in one of his pockets and it was a can of beer. Generally, that's…you know from time to time people will try to sneak alcohol in there, and so we are, we pretty much survey what they're wearing when they come in or any luggage they bring in. He had a can of beer in his pocket, which was poured down the drain and the can was then destroyed."

"You say he passed out and you had to dress him. Did you have any other conversation with him, and take any information?"

"We couldn't get any information from him originally. In fact, since Jack brought him over, we asked Jack to give us a call, but we didn't get a Social Security number for Title 20, or birth date, and those types of things. He was too inebriated to even sign on the line. He was incapacitated."

"Could you smell any smell on him?"

"Yes, there was a smell of alcohol on his breath."

"Okay, anything else you observed about him other than he was ill and the smell of alcohol and passed out?"

"Generally, that's it."

"That was enough?"

"Yeah."

"How long did he remain in your care?"

"He was in our care…well, I got off at seven o'clock. He was still there when I came back the next night. And then, or I didn't work the next night, I believe, looking back over this. I don't see my handwriting for the next night, and then he was picked up at 10:30 in the morning."

"Was there at any time he mentioned maybe to you, that he had experienced food poisoning?"

"No."

"Did you smell any mouthwash on his breath."

"No, I didn't, but mouthwash is alcohol. That has a high content of alcohol in it, so there would, you know…I didn't smell any mouthwash, though."

"Can you drink mouthwash?"

"Yeah, yeah, people do drink mouthwash."

"Do people that you've processed through your facility drink mouthwash for its alcohol content?"

"Shaving lotion…sterno…rubbing alcohol."

"Your answer then is yes?"

"Uh, yes."

"No further questions."

Now it was Mr. Criss's turn to ask questions.

"This can of beer that you found in the jacket. What kind of beer was it?"

"I believe it…of course this was two months ago, and I think it was a Schlitz."

"All right, was it a malt liquor, though?"

"No, I heard Jack say that he did find a malt liquor, but I believe it was a Schlitz. I remember the odor as it was poured down the drain, and thinking that, you know, I destroyed the can because I didn't want it to provide any temptation for anybody else in there. And I do remember the odor."

"All right, you destroyed the can?"

"Right."

"Therefore in doing so, you had to physically touch the can, and you remember it as being Schlitz beer?"

"Yes. That is what I recall."

"Now, you're a technician?"

"Right."

"Did you test Mr. Mitchell's blood or breath or anything like that?"

"We don't test blood. Generally, situations like this don't occur."

"All right, what other substances are there that can smell like alcohol?"

"Any substance that has alcohol as a base."

"All right, if it doesn't have alcohol as a base, can it smell like alcohol?"

"Um, you know, I'm not an expert."

Mr. Spahr said, "Judge, I'm going to object to the question. I'm not sure that he's an expert in such matters. He says he's a technician, but he doesn't say what sort of technician."

"He can answer if he knows."

"I don't know."

"Have you ever had anything like a rum flavored candy?"

"I'm sure I have at one time or another."

"Okay, you've never had the opportunity to smell any kind of flavored candy on one of your client's breath?"

"It's kind of a ludicrous question, because people come to us, when they've been eating rum flavored candies. You know, it's alcohol, so I assume that rum flavored candy would smell like alcohol. I have no way of knowing, though."

"No further questions."

"Nothing," said Spahr.

The Judge asked, "You've been around alcohol and alcoholics for how long?"

"A year."

"Have you ever had an opportunity to compare the smell of something like beer with the smell of 190 proof alcohol or something that's almost straight ethanol?" the Judge asked.

I was wondering if he was trying to gain personal knowledge of alcohol and what a person could drink and not have someone else detect it on ones breath.

"Um, primarily cheap wine. Cheap wine has a distinctive odor to it."

"When you say alcohol then, are you telling me that you've smelled alcohol, or…"

"I'm smelling the odor."

"Not the alcohol that it's made of?"

"No. Alcohol, all different kinds of alcohol, they all have a…they do have a different odor and they don't. It's just…I would assume that primarily depends upon the person, but you know, there is no doubt…there is that smell, that odor that you can definitely pick up."

"Okay."

"Especially because we spend…every hour we go back and run vitals, and after you've had the umpteenth guy breathing in your face, after you've taken vitals."

"You know it's not mouthwash?"

"Yes."

"Okay, you can step down."

"Just a quick question on that, Judge. What, for instance, does a person smell like who's been drinking Everclear, which is 190 proof?" asked Mr. Criss.

"I have no idea. It's not the type of thing where they have, you know, different levels of smell, it's just this overpowering odor. It's distasteful to me, and that's why it sticks in my mind as something that is unpleasant as part of my job."

"All right then, what you're answering is, a person who has drunk half a bottle of Everclear at 190 proof, and someone who has sipped half an ounce of Gillion is going to smell the same because they both contain alcohol?"

"I'm not saying that. What I am saying is that the people that I see where I work at, generally manifest an overpowering odor of alcohol, and I cannot tell you what one person has been drinking, you know, whether it's cheap wine or 190 proof Everclear."

"All right, so what you're testifying to is in a broad spectrum of things?"

"I would have to…"

"Yes or no?"

"Yes."

"No further questions?"

"Nothing, your Honor. The State rests," said Spahr.

"You may step down."

"Mr. Criss, do you have anything else to present?"

"No, your Honor. We rest."

"Any arguments?" the Judge asked.

Mr. Spahr stood. "Judge, I believe the evidence is overwhelming that he has violated the terms of his probation. The Court made specific orders that he was not to drink any alcoholic beverage. I don't think there's any doubt at all that he ignored, for whatever reason, the Court's order. He was previously sentenced to five years under plea agreement. Probation was imposed, and he has failed to live up to his probationary terms. We feel that he should be revoked from probation and ordered to the Department of Corrections to serve the balance of his time. That's all."

"Mr. Criss."

"Yes, in finding, your Honor, I think this is a very weak case by the State. They didn't bring anybody who allegedly drank."

"WHAT?" the Judge sounded shocked.

"With Mr. Mitchell. All we have…we don't even have testimony that in their opinion he was intoxicated. We don't even have testimony that says in their opinion he was drinking. All they say is that he smelled like alcohol. Yet we…"

"Let me save you time. I'll let you make final arguments on what the sentence ought to be, because I don't think there's any question that he violated his terms," the Judge said.

"I want to be heard on the ultimate disposition, if you're finding is that he did drink."

"The finding is that he did drink."

"He didn't have to be intoxicated. He just had to drink an alcoholic beverage," Spahr added.

"Or have it in his possession," commented the Judge.

"Right."

"That will be the finding of the Court. Mr. Spahr, do you want to be heard on sentencing?"

"I think I already made an argument for sentencing, Judge"

"Mr. Criss, do you have any evidence to present prior to sentencing?"

"Yes, I'd like to read the letter that was tendered to the Court by Adam."

"Please don't. I read it shortly before hearing. I will show it as part of the record."

"Thank you, your Honor. We'd like to move for introduction of the letter written by Adam Mitchell, received by the Court."

"State has no objections."

"Yeah, when I received it I did not read it. When I was made aware that it could be something that was going to be discussed today, I decided I'd read it to save us some time," said the Judge.

Mr. Criss was at least trying. "All right, thank you. Now, as far as disposition is concerned, this impresses me as a case where Adam Mitchell has a problem with alcohol, initially, as well as today. And it seems to me the Court has done quite a bit as finding options available to treat that alcohol, but I do find fault in what the Court has taken as it's opinions. And it seems to me that the Court has been very careful to treat Adam Mitchell with kid gloves and has not sentenced him to a hard core program where it's either make it or break it."

Mr. Criss was on a roll, he continued. "Okay? We have a couple of halfway houses and we have Central State, which is a good program. But what I'm suggesting is that the Court modify and give Adam Mitchell one more chance, which is Richmond State Program. Now, the reason I say that is because we all know that nobody from this county has ever satisfactorily completed Richmond State, and it's a make it or break it program. The longest I know that

213

anybody has ever gone through that program from Miami County is three weeks...chose to walk away. Now, I told Adam Mitchell, and Adam Mitchell knows, and if the Court grants him that option, that is his last option. And if the Court wants to send him to Richmond, based on prior experiences from this county, that may be the last option that he will ever be granted, because if he's not gonna make it, we're gonna know within the first three weeks. And if he does make it, then that satisfies what the Court initially told him that was what it wanted him to be, and that is a reformed good citizen. Okay? He may be down there three weeks. He may be down there six months or nine months or maybe longer, but if he comes back and is cured, then we got the ultimate end results. If we send him to prison now, he's gonna be out in another thirteen months. But his problem is not going to be cured. He may be back in prison. And unfortunately, then, he'll have a prior felony, which would be nonsuspendable. So what I'm saying is, Richmond State is the toughest program in the state. We know that nobody's ever successfully completed it in this county. Give him a chance. They're gonna break him down and gonna build him back up. Okay? And if he breaks down to the point where he walks away or he gets busted out of the program, then you will not see me in here arguing for anything. All right? Because this is the only option I know of for the Court. Central State is kind of a kid glove program, individual counseling. Richmond State is a group program. It's just like basic training, I suppose, when they break you down. They don't treat you individually. It's a last step. If he fails there, then he deserves to go to prison. But I think you ought to give him that one opportunity, because that whole history of this case shows that it's been alcohol related. All the treatment, initial reason he came to Court, and his final act. I'm not saying he deserves that final option, but I'm saying I think you ought to give him that option. And I'm not saying this because, yeah he's gonna make it. Let's just see if he does make it. No one else has. Maybe he'll be the first. And I don't know of any candidate...I take that back, I have known of other individuals who have needed Richmond State perhaps more, but I think Adam Mitchell needs Richmond State as much as they do. Let's see if he makes it."

"Mr. Mitchell, is there anything you want to say to the Court before the Court imposes sentence?"

"No, thank you."

"Let's review what's happened in this case. During the course of this matter, the Court allowed Mr. Mitchell to be placed at the St. Vincent's Stress Center. There was treatment given there. At the time of sentencing, the Court made it clear, contrary to what Mr. Mitchell would have us believe in his letter, that for the next two-and-a-half years he would not go home. Do you remember that? That was stated very clearly. It's all in the record. When I suspended the sentence and placed you on probation, and I informed you that in doing that I was not sending you home. Do you recall that?

"No. The only thing I recall is talking to my attorney out in the hallway."

"Well, it was said in Court; it was made very clear; it's all in the records. It was reported by the media, who could have only gotten that out of the hearing, because it's the only knowledge they had. I don't know what I could have done to make it any more clear that the five years suspended sentence did not mean that you were simply going to go home. I indicated to you, and to the entire world, that for the next two-and-a-half years, you would not go home. In fact, in two of the programs you've been in, you've gotten weekend passes. At least two of the programs. So, we've had St. Vincent's Stress Center, then we've had Genesis House, then we had Central State Hospital, and 13th Step House. I'm convinced after a year and two months of trying, that what is missing is not treatment. I don't think we're gonna get anywhere Adam, until two things happen. Number one, when you accept the responsibility for what you did. You killed a state trooper; and number two, when you accept the responsibility for you own actions, and that is that you are an alcoholic and a substance abuser. Then, and only then, are we going to start seeing some improvement in you."

The Judge continued. "That letter is sick. That letter is a denial of any problems. You wrote that like a Harlequin tragedy. Those schmaltzy little stories that housewives read when they feel the need to be depressed, or whatever they do. That's just…that's ramblings of someone who is not accepting responsibility. You are not accepting the responsibility for you. You're now an adult. And until you realize that, and you quit making excuses for yourself and feeling sorry for yourself, nothing is going to change. There's no sense in wasting any more time with any treatment until you make that decision. And once you do, you've had the background. You've had the treatments. You know what you need to do. So you make the decision that you're going to straighten your life out and you will. Until then, it doesn't matter where you are."

I thought the Judge was finished and he started in again. "And after fourteen months of trying, I'm tired of it. Now, the one thing I'm gonna teach you is that there are consequences. Because what I am going to do is revoke your probation and send you to the Department of Corrections. You have earned that. To the extent that you have earned it, I'm going to see that you get it. You have no one to blame for this but you. You can't blame your mother. You can't blame the system. You can only blame yourself. Because for the last fourteen months, this system has tried very hard to straighten your life out. I caught a lot of grief for not sending you to prison the first time."

Adam spoke up. "Can I say something? The programs I've been in, each one of them...the first one was St. Vincent's Stress center, and they were preparing me to go home. The relations I would have to have with my family and when I got back into life. I have not, by not, by no means in any treatment center, been prepared or even talked about going into another city and starting all over. I was down at, um, Central State. My counselor talked to me four times in almost 80 sessions. I went to everybody I could talk to, to see if they could help me, because I thought, I guess, I'd been through a lot. But there's no one that I'd been able to talk to that has helped prepare me for any of this."

"What did you do in the other 80 sessions, or the other 76 remaining?" Judge Embrey asked.

"There was absolutely no individualized counseling. The only thing they had was six to eight people in a room and he talked to those people."

"And they talked to each other?"

"And they talked back to him."

217

"That's called group therapy, isn't it? You had 80 of those sessions?"

"They talked to that individual and did their life history or whatever, and he wanted to accomplish mine in the last four days."

"You were in eighty group therapy sessions, is that correct?"

"Yes."

"Were you permitted to say anything during those sessions?"

"Yes, whenever he talked to me. I, um, when I went into staffing to leave, they asked me what I had learned. And I couldn't come up with anything. I've learned about alcohol and everything, but that isn't the root of the problem here. The root is I'm having problems with reality, with this accident. I can't look at that stuff. And when I have to deal with that, and I don't have anybody to turn to or to talk to, there has to be some release somewhere. I...like when I was first in jail, I spent two months of my life trying to convince myself that this was unreal, because every time I thought about it, I thought I was gonna go nuts. Now that's the whole point. You know, I think he's trying to tell you that I do need help. You know, but I can't change my life in 49 days, or two weeks going to a shrink."

"I'm looking at fourteen months worth, Adam. And I don't think there is anything else we can...I say it again, I do not think you've accepted the responsibility for what's happened. I do not think you're taking responsibility for your life. You're telling me you were in 80 group sessions. Now this is not a perfect world, and there is no perfect alcohol program any place, and there's not one where the prescription is precisely for a young man who is 19 years old and got involved in an alcohol related accident in which a state trooper was killed. Now what you're telling me is that you want a program that particularly fits your exact circumstance, and I'm sorry, there isn't one. We have lousy treatment programs in this state, I have no question about that. The fact that I tried twice to get you into Richmond State Hospital and, instead, the second time, is a witness to that. This state does not do much about rehabilitation. And I'm not one who will pretend that it does, despite the protestation that come out of Indianapolis to the contrary. The fact remains that you have been in two treatment programs, you've been in two halfway houses, and your response is still when the pressure is on to go get drunk. And I'm telling you that we have...at the date of sentencing, we had a very clear understanding, or at least I sure had one, and you were sitting there listening, that if you violated your terms, you were going to prison. Now, they've been violated once, and we ignored it. The second time I'm not going to ignore. I've had it. There is nothing else I can do for you until you accept your responsibilities. Once that happens, I think you may start making some changes. I'm not going to sit here and debate with you at this point. I'm going to revoke the probation, I'm going to order you transported to the Department of Corrections. I will give you credit for the time you spent at the Miami County Jail, at the Genesis House and at the 13th Step House. You were not at the St. Vincent's Stress Center in an incarcerated status. That was something you went to voluntary. The Court released you from jail to allow you to do that. I do not believe you're entitled to credit time for that. We will, in computing the days to which he is entitled to credit, we will add the days that you spent in programs that I itemized, and show it as if you had spent those days in jail. That will leave you with approximately one year and four months to serve, I believe. One year and three months, something along that line. I would suggest to you that after you're out of prison, you might want to recontact the people at 13th Step House and see if they're still interested in taking you. I will not order it again. If you want to go, that's up to you. But, son, this letter has 'I'm not responsible' written all over it. And until you change that mental attitude, nothing's going to happen. Nothing productive will come of your life. You seem to enjoy living at this tragedy. And you're the only one that can change that. That is the order of the Court."

"Thank you, your Honor," said Mr. Spahr.

# Chapter 24

The days turned into weeks and the weeks turned into months. I could only see Adam every other Sunday for two hours at his new place of incarceration. So, my life went from day to day, selling real estate, writing letters to Adam and making the long drive to visit him every other Sunday. It was September again and my day to visit fell on Adam's birthday.

I parked the car, walked to the gate to be let in and made my way to the building designated for visitation. I was accustomed to the ritual. Putting my purse in the locker, I wondered about the other parents I saw waiting to see their sons. The guard unlocked the door and escorted Adam to a table.

"How's my birthday boy?" I asked.

"I'm fine. I'll bet you can't guess who came to see me this morning?"

"Did Jenny come to see you?" I asked.

"No, Dad came to see me. At first I thought he came because today's my birthday...but he never wished me a happy birthday. I don't think he even remembered that it was my birthday."

"Well, at least he came to see you, Adam."

"Mom, the reason he came to see me is because he wanted me to know that he is getting married."

"I know, Adam. He called me one afternoon to tell me he was getting married. I'm afraid I didn't respond very well. I was hurt that he just walked away and left us and let us deal with all of the legal problems and didn't get any

221

emotional support from him at all. I know in my heart that I will always love him, or at least love the man I once knew. But, I don't understand him. I guess that's how some people act when they don't know what to do they just walk away."

"Mom, it was like a slap in the face for him to come here and not remember that it was my birthday. It's like I don't matter to him at all."

"Adam, honey, please don't be upset. I'm sure he thought that he was doing the right thing by telling you. I thought you would be happy that he came to see you at all." I thought of another time, not too long ago that he wouldn't go to see Adam in the Peru jail because there was a square dance and he said going to visit Adam in jail would, *just mess up his Sunday afternoon.* "Please, Adam, just count your blessing and think of something else to talk about."

His eyes were wet and he was just before crying. "I know, I wanted to tell you something. You probably don't know this, but I worry about you aging. I don't know why, but I just can't see you getting old. Anyway, I was reading an article in a magazine and it said if you use Preparation H on your face it would prevent wrinkles, and I want you to try it."

"No way, Adam! I'm not falling for that. If I started using Preparation H on my face the next time I came down here you would tell me I look like someone rear end."

We both started laughing so heartily that people turned their heads to look at us. *That's better*, I thought.

"We both needed that laugh, right, Adam?"

"Mom, did I tell you that I wrote to Judge Embrey and asked for a copy of my trial transcript?"

"No, Adam, you didn't tell me that."

"Well, I did and I got a letter back from him saying that I couldn't have it. Some of the guys in here say it's a public record and I should be allowed to have a copy. They seem to think that there was something funny going on or he would have sent me a copy like I asked him to."

"Well, Adam, I've always thought something wasn't right. I just had a gut feeling and I don't know enough about things like this so I never said anything. Are you sure that you have the right to the transcript?"

"Everybody that I talked to says that I have. Makes me wonder why they don't want me to have it."

"Well, I tell you what. It makes me wonder, too. I'll see if I can find someone who will get it for me. It might take me awhile, but I'll find a way to get it. I promise!" I decided to switch subjects.

"Jenny really likes beauty school. She's making good grades and I think she acts a little happier," I said.

"I'm so glad she's there with you, Mom. She's had a pretty bad time and she deserves to be happy."

"I know, honey, you both do."

The bell rang and it was time for me to leave.

"I'll see you in two weeks about the same time. Take care of yourself and I'll see what I can find out about the transcript okay?"

Adam returned to the door where the guard was waiting and waved goodbye.

My imagination took over and all the way back to Kokomo I tried to think of a way to get a copy of the transcript. "There must be a way to get a copy of the transcript." I said out loud. "I wonder why Judge Embrey doesn't want Adam to have a copy of it. That just makes

223

me more determined. Tell me I'm not going to get something and I'll show you that I will."

# Chapter 25

A few days passed and I got a call from my younger sister Tess.

"Mama won't let us take her to the doctor. She's been in bed for four days and she won't eat, I'm worried about her."

"Tell her that if she doesn't let you take her that I'm coming down there and I'll take her even if I have to call an ambulance," I threatened.

"That might do it. She knows you'd do that very thing. I'll tell her."

"No, put her on the phone and I'll tell her."

I could hear my mother groan then heard a weak, "Hi, there."

"Mama, you know how much I love you. I can't stand to know that you need to go to a doctor and won't let Tess take you. I can tell by your voice that you are in pain. What happened?"

"I don't know. We went to Chattanooga over the weekend and when I got back I was tired. After I went to bed to rest I just didn't have the strength to get up again."

"Mama, please let Tess take you to the doctor or I will be down there to take you myself."

"No, honey, please don't come down here for me. You have enough to worry about. I'll let Tess take me tomorrow. I promise."

"Okay, Mama, you take care of yourself. I love you. Now let me talk to Tess."

"Okay."

"Tess, after you take her to the doctor I want you to call me. I can't work and worry about Mama. I want you to call me immediately after you see the doctor, okay?'

"I'll call. Are you going to be at work?"

"No, I'm going to wait here until I hear from you," I said.

"I'll talk to you in the morning."

I let out a sigh. My gut had the same feeling of dread that I had experienced before. The groaning I heard was still echoing in my head. Anyone who groaned like that had to be in excruciating pain.

I awoke early and tried to do a few things around the house. "Just keep busy" was my motto, as though keeping busy was going to make everything better.

I went upstairs to wake Jenny.

"Good morning."

"I hope you don't mind getting up a little early. I want to talk to you before you leave for school. Come down as soon as you get dressed."

"Okay. Is something wrong?"

"I hope not, Jenny. We'll talk as soon as you're ready for school."

I sat in my cozy breakfast nook with it's yellow-gold checked wallpaper with a colorful fruit border and white lace curtains. I recalled how ugly the house had been before Clay and I had redone it. I loved that house almost as much as I had loved Clay, and wondered about the day I would have to give it up, too.

It wasn't long until Jenny appeared still a little sleepy-eyed, in the breakfast nook.

"What's going on, Paige? I know that worried look. Is it Adam?"

"No, Jenny, it's my mother. I got a call from my sister last night and I could tell that my mother's in a lot of pain. My sister is taking her to the doctor this morning and she's going to call me as soon as she knows something. You know how I am, I just have a bad feeling about this and I was just wondering if I could depend on you to take care of things around the house for me if I have to make a trip to Georgia?"

"Of course I will. After all you've done for me, you don't even have to ask. I'll do anything I can to help you. What's wrong with your mother?"

"I'm not sure, but she sounded bad, and I could hear her moaning just to talk on the phone. She sounded like she was in excruciating pain. I'm going to stay home this morning and call Brian at the office and tell him what's going on just in case I have to leave. If I have to drive to Georgia I'm going to leave today. I probably won't be here when you come home today. I really have a bad feeling, Jenny."

"Jenny sat her coffee down and put her arms around me. "It's going to be all right. Try to be more positive, okay?"

"I'll try, Jenny, but I know this feeling. I've had it before."

Jenny left for school and I called Brian and filled him in on what was going on.


The phone rang.

"Hi, it's me," Tess said.

227

"They put Mama in the hospital immediately. The doctor doesn't have any idea, or at least that's what he's saying."

"I'll be leaving within the hour. Did you call Dorothy?"

"I haven't yet. I called you first. I did talk to her last night and she wants to come home, too. I think she wants you to pick her up. I'll tell her to call you immediately if she wants to ride down here with you."

"Thanks, Tess. Tell Mama I'm on my way. I'll see you soon."

I retrieved my suitcase from the basement and began packing. It was only a matter of minutes before the phone rang again. I knew it would be Dorothy.

"Hello."

"Hi! I was wondering if I could ride home with you?"

"Of course you can. I'm packing now and I have to call my office and run by the bank, then I'll be on my way. I'll be there in about three hours."

"I'll be ready," Dorothy said.

I called my office, left a note for Jenny, and gathered up my things. I loaded them in the car. As I backed out of the driveway, I was praying that I could get to Georgia before anything happened to my mother.

# Chapter 26

It was mid September and the heat of summer was leaving.  Some of the trees were starting to turn colors, and the cornfields were beginning to turn brown.  I loved Indiana in the fall of the year.  The days were still warm and the nights were cool enough for a sweater.

It was different from my childhood in Georgia.  There, it smelled of fresh salt air, with Spanish moss hanging heavily from the mighty oak trees.  Some homes, where the house was in complete shade, had azaleas encircling the house like a flowering wreath placed around a candle. I was lost in my childhood homeland, remembering the days I spent on the beach with Sally, my best friend, all the times we went roller-skating together, and the time that the tide had gone out and left a school of fish in a small tidal creek.  The two of us had scooped the fish up with crab nets.  A man walking by was excited to see what we were doing. We had given him the fish we had gathered from the creek.

I could imagine the sound of the foghorn from a ship far out at sea and could feel the fog so moist that it made my hair wet. That's how it felt to me in Georgia in the winter. Heavy fog, dampness that cooled your skin, and hot coffee to warm you on those winter days on Tybee Island.

I looked up as though I had been somewhere else.  I couldn't believe it. I was in Cincinnati. *How does your mind do it?* I asked myself. Drive and not be aware of the miles you're covering and then suddenly find yourself where you needed to be.

I saw my older sister Dorothy standing in the doorway of her house as I pulled into the driveway. Cincinnati was just far enough South that the signs of fall hadn't begun to show there as much, and it still looked a lot like summer. I got out of the car and greeted my sister with a hug and entered her home.

"I fixed us something to eat. I thought you would be ready for lunch when you got here."

"That's great, and it looks better than the food you get on the road. What do you think is going on with Mama?"

"I don't know. I just know that Tess is very concerned and seems to think it's something really bad. They have Mama in the hospital and they're talking about doing an exploratory operation. I personally don't think there's anything wrong with her. She does things like this for attention."

"Tess didn't tell me that!"

"I know she didn't want you to be alone when you heard it. I told her not to tell you. I knew it would upset you and we have a long drive ahead of us. I'll drive for awhile when we leave here and you can take a break. You made really good time getting down here."

"It's funny, but I don't remember part of the trip. I got to thinking about Tybee and how different it is in Indiana and the next thing I knew, I was in Cincinnati."

"You've had a lot on your mind lately. Look at it this way: it's better to be thinking of something pleasant than to be bored driving. By the way, how's Adam doing?" Dorothy asked.

"I saw him on Sunday and Clay had been there. It was Adam's birthday and Clay forgot it. He just came to see Adam to tell him he's getting married again. I think Adam

230

told me that his Dad was planning to be married on the twenty-second of September. Adam was really hurt that Clay didn't remember his birthday."

"How do you feel about him getting married so soon after the divorce?" Dorothy asked.

"To be honest with you I feel hurt, I don't know why. It's just that he's still out having fun and meeting new people and I'm taking the responsibility of Adam and the lawsuits.

"Have you ever thought about calling Jack?"

"I think about him a lot, but I haven't been in contact with him for awhile and I wouldn't feel right asking him to share this kind of a problem. Adam and I will make it. It's Mama I'm worried about right now."

We continued eating our lunch and as soon as we were finished we cleaned away the plates, secured Dorothy's house, threw her suitcase in the trunk, and left on our trip to Georgia.

# Chapter 27

It was early morning when we arrived at the hospital, too early for visitors. We went to intensive care and found Tess asleep in the waiting area. Dorothy gently shook her.

"Hi, what time is it?"

"It's two in the morning," Dorothy said.

"How's Mama doing?" I asked.

"Not too good. I didn't want to be the one to tell you this. They did the exploratory this afternoon and just sewed her back up. She's full of cancer and there's nothing they can do."

We all cried together in each other's arms. I cried until I thought I was going to be sick. After we had all blown our noses and wiped away the flood of tears, I asked. "When can we see her?"

"They will only let one person in every two hours," Tess said.

"Then why don't you go home and get some sleep? We'll stay here the rest of the night. We've had too much coffee to sleep. How'd Daddy take the news?"

"He's doing pretty well. I think he was like me. He expected something, but not like this. She's been in a lot of pain."

"Did the doctors say how long she has?" Dorothy asked.

"They don't have any idea, but they didn't think it would be too long," Tess answered.

"Why don't you go home with Tess and I'll stay here with Mama," I said.

"Will you be okay here by yourself?" Tess asked.

"I'll be find. You two go home and be there when Daddy wakes up and I'll stay here until Daddy comes back to the hospital."

The two of them left and I sat in the waiting room that had a view of the intensive care unit, watching the nurses go from one bed to another checking the patients in the circular room. I could see part of the bed that my mother occupied and I sat wishing I could go in and see her.

When the time came for me to see Mama for a few minutes I wasn't sure Mama even knew I was there. She would fade into and out of consciousness. I held her hand and stroked her hair like I had done so many times as a child. If Mama had a headache she would lay across the bed and I would sit on the floor and brush her hair for what seemed like hours. Now time had aged us both and I still felt like the little girl who was brushing her mother's hair, as she laid in intensive care at Memorial Hospital.

The nurse announced that time was up and I went quietly back to the waiting room where I sat and waited until the next time, when I could see her for a few more minutes.

The next time she was asleep so I just sat at the bed and held my mother's hand. It was late morning when my father showed up.

"Hey," Daddy called to me. I quickly arose and grabbed my father. "How ya doing, Daddy?"

"I'm okay. Just taking it a day at a time. I knew she was hurtin', but I never thought it would be cancer."

"We'll all be here for you, Daddy. It shouldn't be long before they will let you in to see her. She has slept most of the time I was here."

"Honey, go to the house and get some sleep. This could have us all worn out before it's over with."

"Is Dorothy or Tess coming in to be with you?"

"They're coming in later. Buddy comes by on his lunch hour and after work. He'll be here in about an hour. I'll be fine. You go home and get some sleep."

"I'll see you this afternoon. I love you, Daddy. If Mama wakes up, please tell her that we're here."

"Okay, see you later."

I walked the long corridors of Memorial Hospital, took the elevator to the lobby. The sun shown brightly. It was like a summer's day. I located my car in the parking garage and headed to my beloved Tybee Island. How good it was to be back home.

My sisters were in the kitchen when I arrived at the family home. "How's Mama?" Tess asked.

"I really don't know much. I got to see her twice. The first time she was in and out of consciousness and the second time she was asleep. I don't think she even knew I was there."

"Are you tired?" Dorothy asked.

"I'm getting there. I think I'll put on my swimming suit and lie on the beach and sleep. Are you two going to the hospital?"

"Yes, we'll be there by lunchtime so we can take Daddy something to eat."

"Okay I'll see you at the hospital later today."

I quickly put on my bathing suit and walked the few blocks to the beach. When I arrived at the beach there weren't many people. The season was over as far as the natives were concerned. School had started and all the vacationers had returned home. I saw a ship far out at sea and couldn't tell if it was coming or going. I spread my towel out and sat facing the Atlantic Ocean. I bowed my head in prayer.

"God, please be with my mother, spare her the suffering of pain. I love her dearly, God, and I don't know how I'll go on without her. Please give me a sign as to how long she has left to be with us. I have Adam to worry about, we lost the baby and now my mother is desperately ill. I don't know how much more I can take. God, give me the strength to continue. Amen."

I wiped away the tears and slowly raised my head. There in the sky were six seagulls flying north toward the Savannah River. I rolled over on my stomach and wondered if that meant six days, six weeks, or six months.

# Chapter 28

I had been in Georgia more than a week and the visitation for Adam was getting close. I had to make a decision. My mother was in a regular room now and she was awake and knew what was going on. As I sat by my mother's bedside I felt the tears welling up in my eyes. No matter how hard I tried, I just couldn't hold back the tears.

"Mama, I need to go back to Indiana for a few days. I'm the only one who goes to visit Adam and I couldn't bear for him to miss a visitation day. It's all he has to look forward to. Will you be okay until I can get back?"

"Honey, I understand. Go and see Adam and tell him I love him."

"I'll do that, Mama. I'll leave early in the morning and I'll be back as soon as I can. I love you, Mama. Dorothy is going to stay here and help Daddy. They'll take good care of you. I'll be back as soon as possible."

I kissed my mother goodbye and ran from the room and tried to get out of earshot before I broke down. There was no way to know if that would be the last time I ever saw my mother alive.

Tess watched as I talked to our mother. She followed me from the room.

"It's okay, Paige, I've broken down and cried several times. We all have to let our feelings out. You just have more to deal with than most people. We'll be here, and if I see that Mama is taking a turn for the worse I'll call you. You know Adam needs you, too."

"I haven't told him about Mama. I have to do that so this won't be such a shock to him when it does happen," I said.

"Are you going to be okay making that drive by yourself?"

"I can do it. I'll leave early so I can be home before it gets too late. I'll be okay. I just hated to say goodbye to Mama…because I don't know if it's the last time I'll see her alive."

"You'll be back before something happens to her. Just be careful on the highway going home."

"I will. I'll see you as soon as I can and don't forget to call me."

"Okay."

I left the hospital, sat in my car, leaned my head on the steering wheel and prayed. "God, please keep Mama alive until I can get back to be with her. Amen."

It wasn't quite daylight when I drove over the Talmadge Bridge that crossed the Savannah River and connected Georgia with South Carolina. I felt pulled between my son and my mother and hoped I could be strong enough to be supportive of both. My heart ached and I wiped tears from my eyes as I drove up highway seventeen.

I was just after dark when I arrived in Kokomo. Jenny wasn't home and the house was dark. I pulled into the garage, gathered my suitcase and unlocked the back door. Making my way through the dark house I sat my things down in the dining room and turned on the lights. A stack of mail was on the table. I shuffled through it until I came upon one from my attorney. I ripped it open.

> *Dear Mrs. Mitchell,*
>
> *I am pleased to inform you that the lawsuit that was filed against you and your homeowner's policy for negligible entrustment has been settled out of court.*
>
> *The Lathers were able to collect under the homeowner's policy. It was a landmark case. Never before had anyone been able to collect from a homeowner's policy because of an automobile accident.*

"One down and one to go! Hip-hip hooray! That's the best news I've had lately." I sorted a stack of letters from Adam and put them on my bed. I showered and slipped into my nightgown and sat on the bed reading Adam's letters until I fell asleep.

I awoke to the sounds of Jenny in the kitchen. Quickly, I made my bed and went to the kitchen.

"Hi, Jenny." I gave her a hug.

"Hi. It's good to have you back. What time did you get in?"

"It was around eight. I went through the mail, took a shower and went to bed. I didn't know how tired I was," I said.

"I'll bet," she said.

"How's things here? How's school going?" I asked.

"School's fine. I really like it."

"Is there something wrong, Jenny?"

"No, everything's fine. How's your mother doing?"

"She seems to be handling it pretty well. I think when a person is in so much pain, she is willing to let go. It's probably harder on my dad than anybody. He sits at the hospital all day long. He doesn't want to leave her side. Looks like I have a lot of catching up to do. I'm going to see Adam today. Do you want to come along?"

"I have a test at school that I need to study for so I'm going out to friends house to study. Maybe next time. Gotta get going. I'll see you later. Tell Adam I said hi."

Jenny was out the door and I sat wondering if there wasn't something that Jenny wasn't telling me. Oh well, I don't need to think about that. I had enough to think about.

I dressed and went to my office, I was surprised to see Brian's car in the parking lot. I hadn't expected anyone to be at the office on Sunday. Brian gave me a hug as soon as I walked into the office.

"It's so good to have you back. I've missed you."

"It's good to be back. I'm going to see Adam today and then I need to get back to work for a few days."

"How's your mother?"

"It's terminal and I don't know how long she has left to live. I need to work and I'm hoping that I can go see Adam today and work for two weeks and then go to see Adam again and then leave and go to Georgia until it's time to see Adam again."

"Boy, you're going to push yourself to the end, aren't you?"

"Brian, I don't know what else to do. I thought driving home that I needed a plan in order for me to survive this. I need to work. I thought if I worked really hard for two weeks, then I could spend two weeks with my mother. I want to spend all the time I can with her, but, I can't neglect Adam. He's still so fragile emotionally. Today I have to tell him that his grandmother doesn't have long to live. All he knows is that she is in the hospital. I didn't want to write to him in a letter and tell him she was dying. I don't know how he'll take it."

"Paige, I'll do whatever I can to help you, you know that. I guess I'm selfish. I've missed you while you were gone and I hate to think you're leaving again in two weeks. I know this is hard for you. Just tell me how I can help."

"Brian, I appreciate all you do now. I guess the best way is just to follow through on any real estate transaction that I have going while I'm gone. That's a tremendous help to me. Being single isn't easy, especially when I need to work to pay the bills."

"I know what you mean. I saw Jenny while you were gone, but she didn't see me. Didn't you tell me that was Adam's girlfriend?"

"Yes, she is."

"Well, she was with some guy, could have been a brother for all I know."

"Could've been," I said.

"Brian, I need to leave now. I'll be back this afternoon and get caught up on the transactions. I'll see you tomorrow."

I was wondering why Jenny had acted so strangely and now I knew. Her brother was much younger than Jenny and I knew it wasn't her brother. She wasn't going to say anything to Adam about this. He had a little more than six months left in prison and he didn't need to deal with anything like Jenny having a new boyfriend.

I was right on time for my visiting time with Adam. How many times had I driven this trip and how many times had I gone through the same routine to get to see him. Now

I sat waiting again for them to bring him in.  The door opened and I waited for Adam to walk to the table where I was sitting.  I stood and gave him an extra tight hug.

"What's wrong, Mom?"

"What kind of a greeting is that?"

"Good try, Mom. Now let's have it. What's wrong?" Adam said.

"It's my mother. She has cancer and there's nothing that can be done." I watched as the blood drained from Adam's face.

"Go ahead and cry, it's okay, I've done my share of crying. I just couldn't tell you in a letter. I needed to be here when you heard it."

"How long does she have?" Adam asked.

"There is no way to know, but I can tell you she's not very good. I want to work for a couple of weeks and then come to see you and then go back to Georgia and stay until it's time to come and see you again."

"Mom, that's too much driving for you. Can't you just go down there and stay with Grandma until it's over?"

"Adam, I have to work. Remember it's where the money comes from."

"I feel so helpless in here. If I were out I would do the work and you could go and be with Grandma."

"Honey, I know you would, and you are down to a little over six months, you can help me when you get out, okay?"

"I'm almost finished getting my GED.  They are going to have a small ceremony for those of us who have passed the test," Adam said, changing the subject.

That seemed to be the only way he could handle a problem, pretend it didn't really exist.  He could think about it later when he was alone in his cell. Right now he felt he has to be strong for my sake. I knew him pretty well.

"How's Jenny doing?"

"I only saw her for a few minutes. She was going to someone's house to study for a test. I think she really likes beauty school and she seems to be a little happier than she had been. She's such a sweet girl, Adam."

"Mom, when you go back to Tybee, please stay with Grandma. You don't have to make a trip back here to see me. I'll be fine. Just please stay with Grandma and tell her how much I love her. And please be careful driving down there. I worry about you driving that far alone."

"I really don't mind it, Adam. I pack me a lunch, fill my thermos with coffee and I only have to stop one time for gas or if I need to use the restroom. I drive it in about thirteen-and-a-half-hours. The mountains are pretty this time of year. When you get out, it'll be springtime and they are pretty then, too, with the mountain laurels and dogwood and redbud trees blooming. Just think about when you get out and we get to go back to Tybee together."

"That's about all I do think about, Mom, is getting out."

"I know. I've left some money for you and I'll write and keep you posted on how Grandma is doing, and I'll be back to see you as soon as I can."

I hugged Adam and didn't look back. It was always so sad to see the stressed look on his face and I felt I was abandoning him every time I had to leave him in the prison. It was still hard to believe that such a caring young man could end up in a place like prison.

As soon as I got in my car I pushed in Helen Reedy's tape and listened to "I am Woman."

The words to that song gave me strength and courage, and I needed strength and courage to get through the next six months until I could return to Tybee with my son.

# Chapter 29

I worked as hard as I could every day and called my father every evening to see how my mother was doing. I couldn't believe the energy I seem to have. Maybe what I had thought was energy was only nervous energy. I raked leaves and thought about how much I loved the house that I was getting ready to put on the market.

Clay hadn't shared my love of the house. We lived in a home that Clay had build with his own two hands and he had at first refused to move into town and had come to me the next day with his decision.

"Hon, I've thought about this all day at work and I know you want to move out of this school district because of what happened to Adam at school and I know the economy isn't as good as it had been and I think you're right. We should sell this big house. I don't need to take care of two and a half acres. That hill has always been a problem in the winter and I decided that it makes sense to move into town. Adam will probably do better in a different school district."

"Thanks, Clay, I appreciate you understanding. Do you want me to make an offer on the house in town?"

"Yes, go ahead and see what you can do."

"The biggest reason I wanted to move was because of the beating Adam took from the principal at school. There has to be something wrong with a principal who will tell a kid that he had been wanting to do that for a long time, and then beat a kid black and blue. I'll always regret not turning him in to the authorities. I should have never gone to the convention and I would have been here when that happened."

"Clay, if you don't want to move, we don't have to. I know how you are and if you didn't want to remodel that house you would be cussing it with every stroke of the hammer. We can just stay here."

"No, Hon, listen to me. It's all right. You're right. It makes sense to make the move for more reasons that one. Go ahead and make an offer on the house. We can use my V.A. loan and do some work on the house before we move in. Okay?"

Clay had such a loving way about him about ninety five percent of the time. The other five- percent always brought me to tears. I couldn't handle that little five percent that made me so angry and I loved the other part of him with all my heart. I must ask Bob Lawson about that five percent. As I raked the leaves I thought about Friday afternoons when I always tried to be home before five o'clock so we could go out and eat. Clay would be on the riding lawn mower, and the minute I pulled into the driveway he would have a big smile on his face and throw up his hand and wave to me. It was like clockwork on Fridays in the summer time. I would come home, he would finish mowing the lawn and come in and give me a kiss and then would ask, "Where would you like to eat?"

"Why don't we go to Mike's for pizza?" I would answer.

"I was thinking maybe we should try the catfish place," Clay would say.

I would look at Adam and wink.

"That's fine."

Adam and I played a game every Friday. Clay always asked where we wanted to go eat and Adam and I would try to guess where he wanted to go. We never did get it right. Clay always asked and then picked where he wanted to go.

I was going to miss this house and all the memories that it brought back to me.

The time came for my trip back to Georgia. I left early and drove into Memorial Hospital parking lot as the sun shone through the orange and purple sky with it last light of the day.

I made my way to my mother's room. A nurse was just coming out.

"How's she doing?"

"To be honest with you, I think she had been waiting for you to come back."

I entered the hospital room and quietly approached the bed.

"Mama, I'm here now." I bent to kiss my mother and saw that she wasn't as bright as she had been the last time I had been there.

"Paige, is that you?"

"Yes, Mama, it's me."

"Thank God, you're here."

"I'll stay with you tonight, Mama."

I pulled a chair up to the side of the bed and held my mother's hand and stroked her hair.

After Mama had gone to sleep I called my parents' house.

"Hello, Dorothy."

"Where are you?"

"I'm here at the hospital. I'm going to stay the night."

"Paige, you need rest, too. You've driven all day and now you're going to stay up there all night?"

"I have to, Dorothy, I don't want our mother to die alone and I have a feeling that the time is almost here. I'll be fine."

"I really think you should come home, Paige. Mama sleeps most of the time. You can go back in the morning."

"I'm going to stay. If anything happens I'll call you," I insisted.

I took my place beside my mother's bed and watched as the nurses came in frequently and suctioned Mama. She groaned in pain with each suction. After the nurse had left the room and Mama was still awake I asked. "Mama would you like for me to pray with you?" She shook her head no.

"Do you want me to say the Lord's Prayer?" She indicated that she did and I prayed. "Our Father which art in Heaven, Hollowed be thy name. Thy kingdom come. Thy will be done in earth as it is in heaven. Give us this day our daily bread. And forgive us our debts, as we forgive our debtors. And lead us not in temptation, but deliver us from evil. For thine is the kingdom, and the glory, forever. Amen.

"Mama I love you so much and I can't stand to see you suffer like this. Do you want them to suction you anymore?"

She shook her head no and the next time the nurses came in I told them not to suction. I prayed silently. *Lord, I'm ready for you to take her home. I will miss her terribly, but I can't stand to see her suffer anymore.*

The gurgling sounds got stronger and I called in a nurse and we both stood and watched helplessly as my mother passed on into death.

The nurse said, "She has been waiting for you to come home."

"I know she has. She's at peace now."

I picked up the phone. It was two in the morning.

"Hello."

"Dorothy it's over. Mama just died."

"Stay at the hospital. I'll be right there."

A nurse led me into a waiting room where I cried until I was sick. My sister arrived shortly.

"Did you tell Daddy?"

"He knew when the phone rang. Tess stayed with him. We'll do what needs to be done here and then go home."


I called Brian the next morning.

"Hello, Brian."

"Hi. How's your mother?"

"She died last night, I thought you would want to know."

"I'm so sorry, Paige. Are you all right?"

"I'll be okay. She was suffering so much, it's easier to accept that she gone. At least now she isn't in so much pain. The funeral is on Sunday. I don't know how long I'll be here."

"Don't worry about it. I'll take care of things until you come home."


The funeral parlor was bustling with people and I was seeing folks I had gone to school with and hadn't seen for a long time. My mother looked peaceful lying there in her coffin. Her long fingernails had been painted and she looked more like herself than she had since she'd had her stroke two years before. We all remembered our mother saying she didn't want people to be sad at her funeral. She wanted us to be happy for her because she had gone to a better place.

Someone came up behind me and touched me on the shoulder. I turned and there stood Brian.

"What are you doing here?"

"I came to be with you," Brian answered.

"I can't believe you found me."

"It's not hard to do."

We held each other in a tight embrace and smiled at each other. I had never had Brian hold me like that before.

After the service in the chapel we drove to Hillcrest Abby for the gravesite service. As they were lowering the coffin into the grave, Rose Thompson, one of my mother's friends came to me and put her arm around me.

"Paige your mother was proud of you, and don't ever forget it. You made her proud," Rose said.

All I could think about was how sad I was, and I just wanted to lie down on top of Mama's coffin and be buried with her. There's nothing like the love of my mother, and she had been my friend, too. I was going to miss her more than anyone would ever know. If it weren't for Adam, I didn't know if I could keep going.

*Lord, I don't know how much more I can take. It would be so much easier to go with my mother. O, God, give me the strength to make it through these next few months so I can come back to Tybee and find some peace within my soul. Please, Lord, please, give me strength.*

After the funeral the women of the church had prepared a meal at our island home. Brian had joined the family gathering and seemed to fit in wonderfully. After everyone had eaten I was getting myself a piece of cake.

"Want a piece of this delicious looking cake?" I asked Brian.

"Sure."

I handed Brian a slice and cut a piece for myself.

"Wow, this is excellent. You'll have to get the recipe, it's delicious. I'll say one thing, the people down here really know how to cook. Everything I had to eat was delicious. I don't know that I've ever had a better meal."

"Does anyone know who brought the this cake over?" I asked.

"I think Mrs. Allifi brought it," someone said.

"You remember her, Paige. She worked at City Hall with Daddy," said Dorothy.

"Where does she live?" I asked.

"Over in Fort Screven next to where Naylor's store use to be. Her husband died several years ago."

"She looked better after he died than she ever did while he was living. Hellava nice lady," Daddy said.

"We'll go over there this afternoon and get the recipe. I'll take you for a tour of Tybee Island," I said to Brian.

One by one people started leaving and by mid-afternoon there was just the immediate family left.

Brian and I excused ourselves and went to locate Mrs. Allifi and her recipe for the delicious cake.

I explained to Brian that Fort Screven was a training camp for the Army and was closed in the mid-nineteen-forties. Mrs. Allifi was living in one of the converted army buildings that she called home. I knocked on the door.

I could watch Mrs. Allifi through the screen door slowly making her way to answer.

"Hi, Mrs. Allifi, I'm Paige Mitchell."

"Come on in. I don't know if I ever met you or not. I used to ride on the school bus with your mother as a helper after I retired from the city and I remember your mother talking about you a lot."

"We came to thank you for the cake you brought to our house and tell you how delicious it was."

Brian said, "I think that's the best cake I have ever eaten. Would you consider giving us the recipe?"

"Sure. I feel flattered when someone wants a recipe. Let me get it for you."

Brian winked at me as Mrs. Allifi went to the kitchen to get the recipe and a card to write it on.

"It's called a Barbara Mandrell Cake. All you do is mix a yellow cake mix according to direction and add one cup of chopped walnuts and drain a can of mandarin oranges, chop them and add those to the mix. After you bake the cake, let it cool and then take a large can of crushed pineapple and add a package of instant vanilla pudding and a cup of Cool Whip. You put the pudding between the layers and on top on the cake and ice the sides with Cool Whip. It's really easy."

"We'll think of you every time we make this cake. We sure do appreciate you giving us the recipe and most of all for bring it to the house for Mama's funeral."

After we left Mrs. Allifi's house I drove directly over to the Tybee Island lighthouse. "What do you think of our lighthouse?" I asked Brian.

"It sure is a tall one."

"It's the tallest one on the East Coast, or at least that's what I've been told. I used to love to climb it and look out over the island. It's beautiful. I don't think I appreciated the beauty of this island when I was a child growing up here. It never dawned on me that every child didn't have a beach to play on and an old fort to explore. I found several bullets and a knife once in the sand around the fort. I wonder what happened to them?

"Well let's go and I'll show you some more sites."

Back in the car I continued, "There have been several movies made around here. 'Gator' is probably the most well known one. Mama said she used to pass Burt Reynolds and Jerry Reed every morning while they were filming the movie. She was driving the school children to school on the bus, and Reynolds and the crew were driving out from Savannah to do their filming. Mama told me that once she saw General Eisenhower at the post office, it seems he had friends down here that lived on the back river that he used to stay with."

"How much do the properties run around here?"

"I really don't know, but the're cheaper than what you think. When I was a kid I can remember people laughing when they found out that I lived at the beach all year long. Back then only the lower class lived on the islands all year. The wealthy only came down in the summer. Some of these big homes are vacant all winter. This area is called Officers Row. The name has hung on since it was a real fort. We still refer to it as Fort Screven."

"How big is the island?"

"I think it's about two miles long and at some places it's only about four blocks wide. If you want to count driving in on the highway, it's probably two miles wide."

"I think you people are sitting on a gold mine and are about fifty years behind times here."

"That's the way we like it! Happiness down here is never having to leave the Island. In the summer time it's bumper to bumper traffic here. The natives go to town during the week and stay off the Tybee Road on the weekend. We better get back. How long will you be here?" I asked.

"I'll be leaving in the morning. I just wanted to be here for you. I need to get home and take care of business for us until you come home. Do you have any idea when that'll be?"

"Not right now. I'll hate to leave Daddy, but I need to get back and visit Adam. I'll come home as soon as I can."

"I can see why you would want to move back to Tybee. It's very peaceful here and, of course, your family is here."

"I think Adam will be better off here than staying in Kokomo. At least here people you know will speak to you and from what I have felt in Kokomo, people I know will walk in the other direction to avoid me. I think they feel like what Adam did was deliberate and that I was the cause of it. Maybe they just don't know what to say. But it hurts, and I don't want to feel like I do. Here no one will know and he can start over."

"I…there's something…never mind."

"What is it, Brian?"

"It's…well, I have left my wife. I moved into a rental house that I owned and I've filed for a divorce."

"I hate to hear that, Brian. Getting a divorce is the worst thing I ever did. I just can't figure out why some people can make it through all those years together, even when there are problems in their lives, yet others can't. I'm sorry."

My sisters were finishing the dishes when we arrived back at the house and then we all gathered on the back porch to reminisce about the good times that we had all had together.

"Daddy, did you ever fix the wallboard in the back bedroom where Dorothy pushed me into it?"

"Yep, I told you when it happened that I wasn't fixin' it until the two of you left home. All you ever did was fight."

No one wanted to comment on that. It has been going on, since I had taken my first breath would be my guess. There's an act that's ongoing on the surface where people think we get along. But in the times that we spend one-to-one I have always come out on the short end of the stick. Once my sister Dorothy beat me until I was black and blue and told me if I told Mama that she would beat me some more. Shortly after the beating I asked Mama to scratch my back and she saw the black and blue marks for herself. I can't recall the outcome, but Mama found out on her own that Dorothy did it. The marks that are left now are emotional ones, not visible to the eye. Another time Dorothy gave me a dress that she had stapled the hem up. I sat and picked all the staples out and then hemmed the dress. I washed and pressed it and hung it on the back of the door so I could wear it to school the next morning. Dorothy took her shower first and when I came out of the bathroom after taking my shower Dorothy had the dress on. I ripped it down the middle so she couldn't wear it. Needless to say that started yet another fight. Of course it was my fault. Dorothy had nothing to do with it.

Brian left early the next morning and I spent the rest of my time being with my father and walking to the beach every evening. Sometimes I cried for my mother and sometimes I cried for Clay and for the baby that I would never know. I wondered if life for me would ever hold the happiness I had known being in Clay's arms during our earlier years together.

One thing was certain: I would stand on my own two feet and never again feel the hurt of a man like I had with Jack and Clay. No one would get that close to me ever again.

I wondered, too, if time would ever erase the memories I had made with Clay every time I heard a train's whistle.

# **Chapter 30**

Arriving back in Kokomo, I jumped right back into my real estate job and did my usual routine of working every day and writing letters to Adam every night.

It was getting close to Christmas again and I received a letter from Adam with some exciting news.

*Dear Mom,*

*The prisons are over crowded and there is talk that some of us short timers are going to get out early. We should know in a few days. I'll write you when I know something.*

*Wouldn't it be wonderful if Adam got out early and we could spend Christmas together?* I felt excited and prayed that Adam would be one of the one's who would be released early.

Every day I hurried home to see if I would get another letter with some more good news.

It was time for a visit to see Adam. Maybe he would tell me when I saw him.

I stopped for a Coke on my way to the prison and listened to my Helen Ready tape during the drive to Putnamville, Indiana.

I could hardly wait for Adam to be let into the room. They frowned on personal contact with the prisoners, so I greeted him with a quick kiss on the cheek before the guard could say anything.

"I've been so excited since you wrote to tell me that they are letting people go early because of the prison's being over crowded. Have you heard anything?"

"No, Mom, I don't know when I'll hear. Sometimes I think they tell us things like that just to get our hopes up. I'm so glad that you're back. How's Grandpa doing?"

"He seems to be doing okay. I think sometimes when a spouse has been sick for a long time like Grandma, death is a relief in the beginning. I'm sure grief and loneliness will take over in time. Aunt Dorothy is there with him and that makes me feel better. I don't know if I could have left him alone. I'm just happy she's there."

"I've been busy with real estate since I've been home. I want to try and make as much money as possible before we move to Georgia."

"Are you going to sell real estate in Georgia?"

"I don't know yet, Adam. We're going to play it by ear. I'll bet you're counting the days, aren't you?"

"Yes, if I have to stay until April 26, I'll have 144 more days left. If I'm one of the lucky ones I could have about 12 days left," Adam said. "How's Jenny?"

"I think she's fine, Adam, she says she's made a lot of friends at beauty school and she goes out more than she used to. I think she's much better than she had been. I work so much I don't see a lot of her. She does leave me notes if she isn't going to be home until later. Doesn't she still write to you?"

"Not like she use to. I'm lucky to get one letter a week."

I feared that Jenny did have a boyfriend, but I didn't think Adam needed to be told that kind of news now.

"I'm sure she's just busy with school and just doesn't have time. Don't worry about it, okay? I'll say something to her and maybe she'll make more of an effort to write to you."

"I got my GED while you were away."

"I'm sorry I couldn't be here for that, Adam."

"It's okay, Mom. Not too many people showed up for the ceremony anyway. I don't think people like coming here for any reason."

"Well, it's not the best place for a visit, but I'd never miss an opportunity to see you."

"I'm one of the lucky ones here. Some of these people never have any visitors. I feel sorry for them. You've only missed one visiting time the entire time I've been locked up. It's meant a lot to me, Mom. I appreciate you being there for me and after I get out I'll be there for you. I don't know how I can ever repay you for all you've done."

"I don't expect any repayment. But I'll tell you what, if it makes you feel any better when I get old you can take care of me then. How'll that be?"

"Mom, I can't imagine you getting old. But I will always take care of you, I promise," Adam said.

"Just say your prayers that you'll get out of here before Christmas. I can't believe that there's a possibility you'll be home for Christmas. It would make me truly happy."

"I'll let you know as soon as I hear anything."

The bell rang and visiting hours was over. Adam returned to his cell to anxiously await any news about being released early.

A few days later the letter I had been waiting for arrived.

*Dear Mom,*

*I thought it was too good to be true. I wasn't one of the people picked to go home early for Christmas. I don't know how they made their decisions, but one man who had bitten the penis off of a small boy was released early so he could be with his family for Christmas.*

*I guess it's like we've said before. It's not so much the crime you commit, it's who's involved that determines the punishment. I remember Diane Monahan telling me when we were going back to the jail after the baby's funeral that the state troopers wanted me to do jail time. I guess they want me in here for Christmas, too.*

*I wonder sometimes if the two girls that insisted that I go with them in Fort Wayne could have been someone that the state police hired to get me drunk. I'll always wonder.*

I couldn't believe that the people in charge would let a man who had bitten the penis off a child would be released early for Christmas and would keep Adam in there. Adam's situation was an *accident*. And biting the privates off of a child was a deliberate act. I felt the heat coming to my face. I guess it's who was killed. Probably the little boy didn't belong to a family of a State Trooper or to some well-known official. I know this is America, but our judicial system sucks. *It's not what you did, it's who you did it to.* How can Adam take so many heartbreaks? He was truly hoping that he would be one of the lucky ones who got out early. I would have to turn to my faith in God to get through yet another disappointment. I circled April 26, 1985 on my calendar. That would be the day of a new life for the two of us.


Christmas morning I was alone. Jenny had gone to spend the holidays with her family.

I got out of bed made myself a cup of coffee and curled up in my overstuffed chair. It had been Clay's chair when he had lived with me and it gave me pleasure just to cuddle up in it. I sat planning our new lives in my mind waiting for Adam to call me. I wondered how many other people were alone on Christmas morning and also if Clay ever thought about me. *Probably not,* I told myself. Why would he think about me when he had a new wife? I thought about my mother and went to the phone to call Daddy.

"Merry Christmas, Daddy."

"Merry Christmas to you, too."

"What's going on down there? Is Dorothy cooking dinner for you?"

"Yeah, Tess and Gordon are coming down and she's bringing me a red velvet cake. It has to be a special occasion for me to get one."

"That's probably because she works baking cakes in her shop all day and doesn't want to bake when she gets home. She does a terrific job on those cakes. Wish I could have a piece."

"I'll freeze you a piece if you want me to."

"No, Daddy, you just enjoy your cake and when Adam gets out I'll have her bake another one. That will be a special occasion. Did you realize that he gets out on what would have been yours and Mama's fiftieth wedding anniversary?"

"No, I didn't. We almost made fifty years. It was forty nine and a half years."

"What was your happiest year together?"

"I think 1936."

"Wasn't that the year you got married?"

"Yep."

It was obvious to me that I wasn't getting any information out of Daddy.

"Is Dorothy busy?"

"She's always busy doing something. Moved my room around and now I can't find a thing."

"Let me talk to her. You have a good Christmas. I love you, Daddy."

"Here's Dorothy."

"Merry Christmas."

"Merry Christmas to you, too."

"How's Daddy doing?"

"You know Daddy. He sits in that chair, looks out onto highway 80, and he knows everything that goes on, on Tybee Island. I don't know how he can see all of that from his chair." She laughed.

"I don't know either, but you're right, he does or thinks he knows everything that goes on."

"Perry comes by to see him and he starts cussing the minute he hears Perry's car in the driveway. Perry comes in and starts talking to him and at first he is really quiet and after a while he gets over his feelings and warms up to Perry and thanks him for coming by.

"The other day Mrs. Markle stopped by. When she left, Daddy said, 'Poor thing, she can't help it she's so ugly, but looks like she could stay home.' I laugh every time I think about it," Dorothy said.

261

"There's nothing quite like Daddy. Is he getting to you?"

"No, if I think that's happening I go to the Desoto Beach Club and have a beer."

"Have you been there very much?"

"About every day!"

"At least you can laugh about it."

"When is Adam getting out?"

"Not until the twenty-sixth of April. I can hardly wait. I'll relieve you of some responsibilities with Daddy when I get there. I need to go. I'm expecting a call from Adam and I don't want to miss it. Give Daddy a kiss for me and tell Tess and Gordon I said Merry Christmas."

"Take care of yourself and tell Adam we all said hello."

*What a way to spend Christmas*, I though. *Home alone and no one to share the holiday with*. I thought about what Dorothy said about Mrs. Markle and started laughing. One thing about Daddy, he called them as he saw them. He was always saying funny things to us as children. I remembered when he asked me as a child, "What kind of a bird is that Paige?" pointing to a bird perched on a post in the back yard.

"I don't know, Daddy."

"It's a mileormore."

"I never heard of a mileormore."

"Well, that bird will stick his bill in the mud, whistle out his butt and you can hear him for a mile-or-more."

I was smiling to myself and thinking about my childhood and how naive I had been, and how much I was looking forward to going back home.

Poor Mrs. Markle. She's actually a very nice lady.

# Chapter 31

The winter days had passed and spring was in the air. I had put my home on the market and was telling myself what I had told clients for years, "Everything will work out like it is suppose to, you just have to have faith." Somehow I wasn't listening to my own advice. I was anxious about the move and having second thoughts about whether or not I was doing the right thing.

Sitting at my desk and going over a file, the receptionist approached me. "An offer just came in for you."

"Thanks, What property is it on?"

I opened the envelope and saw that the offer was on my own property. It was less than I wanted and I needed to call the mortgage company to see what my balance was so I could figure the other expenses before I could make a decision. Possession would be a problem, too. I didn't want to give it up until after Adam got out of prison. My mind was spinning. Lots to think about. It was getting too real for me. I loved that house and now I had to make a finial decision about selling it. I would ask Brian what he thought. He was a good businessman and his judgment wouldn't be clouded as mine was. Many memories were there for me to let go of, good and bad.

I knocked on Brian's office door.

"Come in."

"Hi. Busy?"

"No, have a seat. What's going on?"

"I just got an offer on my house and I'm not sure what I should do with it."

"That's just like a realtor, you can tell other people what to do but you can't make a decision. Let me see the offer," he said laughingly.

I sat quietly while Brian read quickly through the offer on my home. As he flipped to the last page I said. "I'm concerned about the possession and also the price. They want the garden tractor included, too. I really can handle this, but so many times you think of things that I don't. I just thought I would ask you what you thought before I countered it." He nodded and passed the paper back to me.

"Do you think it will appraise close to the asking price?" I asked.

"I don't know why it wouldn't, you did comps on it before you put it on the market, didn't you?"

"I did, but there wasn't much to compare it to. You can't find many homes with more than an acre in the middle of a sub-division. That was the original home on the farm before it was subdivided into Terrace Meadows. So much of what I came up with was on a Swag."

"Well, you're really good at Sophisticated Wide A— Guesses. I'd counter it at whatever price you want and change the possession to when you want to move out, or you could go with a delayed closing. That's probably what I would do. Delay the closing until 30 days before you want to be out and that way you won't be paying any rent. Then offer to sell him the garden tractor."

"That sounds good. I need to do a net sheet before I make a counter offer so I'll know how much I'll have."

"Got time for lunch?"

"Sure. Let's go, I'm hungry."

"How's Doc's sound?"

"It sounds good to me. I might even have a piece of their coconut cream pie," I said.

Once at the restaurant, Brian said, "What are you going to do about Jenny?"

"She can stay there until I'm ready to move out. She's almost finished with beauty school. She's never said what she plans to do when she finishes school. I just assumed that in time she and Adam would get married.

We finished lunch and drove back to the office. Brian had never had a good opinion of Jenny and that bothered me.

When I returned home, Jenny was in the living room.

"Hey, Jenny guess what! I got an offer on the house."

"Wow, Paige, that is great. So, what are you going to do?"

"Well, I think I am going to delay the closing until 30 days before Adam is released. That way we can stay here until we leave and not have to pay rent anywhere. Have you thought about what you're going to do after beauty school, or do you and Adam have any plans?"

She paused for a moment "Paige, I've been meaning to talk to you for awhile now. A few months ago my girlfriends and I were out, and I kind of met this guy Derek, from the air base. I wasn't looking to meet anyone, but things have gotten serious."

She paused again and looked at the floor.

"He wants to get married, Paige," she said with tears in her eyes.

"I never meant for things to happen this way, honestly. I was just waiting for Adam to get out, then I thought things would be okay. I am really sorry."

Jenny wasn't half as sorry about this as I was. How much more could Adam take? I knew how much emotional turmoil I felt with the accident, my divorce, the baby dying and my mother's death. Could Adam handle another serious emotional turmoil?

"Well, Jenny, all I can say is that all things work out the way God intended for them to. Are you planning to tell Adam?"

"Yes, Derek and I talked about it, and he is willing to drive me down to talk to Adam about it. I know I need to do it."

I went to see Adam on the next visiting day hoping that Jenny had kept her word and had told Adam about her plans.

I waited, as did the other visitors, until they allowed a few men at a time into the visiting area. Adam always smiled when he saw me. He was looking more like a young man now than a teenager. He had to be more than six feet tall and his red hair was cut close to his head allowing his high cheekbones to be more prominent. His blues eyes seemed to dance with excitement when he walked toward me. I gave him a quick hug before anyone could stop me and quickly took a seat on my side of the table. I could understand the rules of the prison. But, I wasn't smuggling drugs to my son. I just wanted to give him a quick hug.

"Hi, honey, how's it going?"

"It's okay. I'm just counting the days until I'm out. Jenny came to see me."

"Are you okay with her getting married?"

"*She's getting married.*" Adam's face was white.

He didn't know. "Adam, I'm so sorry. Jenny said she was coming down here to tell you. I thought you knew." His eyes were wet and I could tell he was fighting as never before to keep his feelings locked tightly inside himself. He couldn't speak. I knew better but I reached for his hand. I had time to give him a touch of understanding before a guard looked our way. It wasn't enough. Adam needed more than a touch from my hand. His heart was breaking and I was helpless. I never knew what to say in moments like these. "Honey, I know you have been through a lot. Remember how you are always telling me that *the trials of your faith are more precious as gold*?"

"Well, I'm feeling pretty rich right now."

How much more could my son endure? He had lost his newborn son, his grandmother and now he had lost Jenny, too. Then there were the things he had to cope with by being in prison. I hoped I lived long enough to see how all of this was going to work out for the best.

"I don't know why she didn't tell me, Mom. She gave me a poem that said something like, *If you love something set it free and if it comes back to you it's yours.* I wondered at the time what that was all about, but she never told me she was getting married. Do you know him?"

"I don't. Brian told me he saw her with a guy while I was in Georgia. I thought it might be her brother, so I didn't think too much about it. I'm truly sorry, Adam. Are you going to be okay with this?"

"Do I have a choice?"

"You've got a point there, Adam. Would you feel better if I promised you I would start using Preparation H on my face?"

Adam broke out in a laugh that could be heard throughout the visiting area. "Mom, you can always make me laugh. You don't have to try the Preparation H."

I suppose that was the way both of us tried to handle our problems. We found something to laugh about and then we didn't have to think about the hurt and the pain the problem was causing us. It became a huge lump in our throat and we continued swallowing until it disappeared into our bodies to join all of the other lumps that we had had to swallow. I, however, had my swallowing container almost full and Adam had to be feeling the same way.

"Just six more weeks and you'll be free, Adam."

"I know, Mom. I count the days."

"Just think about how nice it's going to be when we get to Tybee. We can go for walks on the beach every evening if you want to."

"There are a lots of things I want to do when I get out. I want you to know when you get older and need someone to take care of you; I'll always be there for you. I can never repay you for all you've done for me."

"That's a deal, Adam, I'll just look at that as the time I can get even."

I left knowing that this would be another one of the days Adam would retreat to his own thoughts to find a way to handle the news that Jenny wouldn't be there for him when he got home.

The counter offer was made and accepted. That meant I had a lot of work to do before moving day. I started cleaning out closets and dresser drawers, cabinets, and the basement, putting everything I didn't want in the garage for a sale. I spent hours each night working on setting up for the sale and packing boxes. I put an ad in the *Kokomo Tribune* for the sale to start on Saturday.

The people had started arriving early and I was glad that Carol had offered to help me. There was no way I could have taken care of all those people by myself. By noon the crowd started thinning out.

"Paige, how about some coffee of tea or something?" Carol called to me.

"Sure, I'll be right out."

I went into the house and fixed the tea when I saw a lady through the kitchen window that looked very familiar. I took the tea out to the garage to Carol and saw the lady up close. I knew her, but couldn't place her. It was embarrassing to forget a client, but I didn't think this was a past client. There was something about those green eyes that looked really familiar. It was as though someone were speaking for me.

"Pardon me, but is your name Faye?"

"Yes, it is. Do I know you?"

"Faye...I'm Paige."

"I would never have know you. I quess age changes us, doesn't it?"

"How are your sons?"

Her eyes became wet and I immediately wished I hadn't asked.

"Jack Lee is in Ohio with his dad and A.J. is dead."

"I'm so sorry, Faye. What in the world happened?" I had done it again. Couldn't I think before I asked such personal questions?

"Come on in here." I motioned Faye into the breezeway of my home.

269

"Would you like some tea?"

"No, thank you."

"I'm sorry I asked you that, Faye. You don't have to tell me."

"It's okay, A.J. killed himself, because Jack wouldn't have anything to do with him. He felt so rejected and Jack was always doing for Jack Lee, but for some reason he just wouldn't accept A.J. as his son. It got to be too much for A.J. and he took his own life. How's your son. Wasn't his name Adam?"

"Yes, his name is Adam and I'm sure you read in the papers about a young man who hit and killed a State Trooper on US 31. Well, it was Adam and he gets out of prison in about four weeks and we're moving south when he gets out. That's why I'm having this garage sale, to get rid of as many things as possible"

"Did Jack ever claim him?" Faye asked.

"I never let Jack see Adam. I married and gave Adam my husband's name. That's the way Clay wanted it. I told him when we got married, if it didn't work out, I would never hold him responsible for Adam. Jack used to call me every time he and his wife had a baby and tell me about it. But he never saw Adam."

"Do you have a picture of Adam?" Faye asked.

"Yes, I do. I'll get it and be right back."

I returned with the picture and handed it to Faye. She stared at it and said. "I can't believe it. He looks just like A.J." She wiped away the tears.

I got up and put my arm around Faye.

"I'm so sorry for what you've had to go through Faye."

"It doesn't sounds like you had a picnic either."

She was getting control of herself.

"I need to go. My husband is expecting me home. I'm glad you said something to me. We do foolish things when we're young and have to live with the results the rest of our lives. I hope things work out well for you and Adam. Ah…could I borrow that picture of Adam?" she asked.

"Why, of course, you can."

"I want to show it to my husband. I'll bring it back to you."

"That's fine. I'm glad we got to see each other. Thanks for stopping."

I returned to the garage and Carol immediately asked, "What was all of that about?"

I told her about Faye and her sons. Carol already knew about Adam.

"What a pity, I always thought that maybe Jack loved her more than he did me. I used to be a little envious. That lady has been through hell. I was much better off walking away and never letting Adam see his real father."

"Yeah, it seems like it." Carol agree.

The mailman had just passed and I walked to the mailbox. It was a letter from Adam. I opened it and was reading as I walked back to the house. They were moving him to Michigan City to be released. Any further correspondence would have to go to Michigan City and that's where I would have to go to pick Adam up.

I found a map in my car and located Michigan City. I had never been there and would have to find out where the prison was located.

# Chapter 32

April 26 finally arrived and I got up early for my drive to Michigan City. I drove north on 31, passed where the accident had happened and this nightmare had started, and then was on my way to pick up my son. How long I had waited for this day!

I found the prison and sat in the car as Adam had told me to. It seemed like hours before I saw him walk through the gate. I got out of the car and waited for him to come to me. We embraced and the tears of joy were running down our faces. My sweet redhead was free.

We arrived home late in the afternoon and Adam was walking from one room to another, so glad to be home.

The doorbell rang.

I open the door to find Faye standing there.

"Hi. Please, come in. We just came home. Adam, come here. I want you to meet the lady I was telling you about."

I watch Faye as Adam entered the room. The tears were there again. *It must be painful for her*, I thought, *to have someone look so much like her deceased son.*

"Faye, this is Adam."

"It's nice to meet you. Mom told me about you."

"Well, I wanted to return this picture, and now I've got to meet you. That's great." Faye said.

"I have a lot of questions I'd like to ask you," Adam said.

"Would you like for me to pick you up for breakfast in the morning, and we can talk? I'm sure your mother has a lot to do, and some of it would be very boring to her."

"Mom?" Adam looked to me for approval.

"That's fine with me, Adam, if that's what you want to do."

"It might be the only chance I have to find out some things about my real father. I want to go with her," Adam said.

"I'll pick you up about eight o'clock then."

"I'll be ready."

After I had closed the door Adam said. "Mom I hope you don't mind. She has such sad green eyes, doesn't she? I just want to talk with her and find out what he was like."

I wasn't sure if he meant his Dad or his deceased half-brother. It was time for Adam to hear whatever he wanted to know. I had protected him from the truth long enough, and Faye would probably know more about his father that I did.

Adam was up and ready when Faye arrived and I continued working on getting the things ready for the movers.

It was late morning with they returned and Faye had dropped him off in the driveway and backed out before I realized that she wasn't coming in.

"How was your breakfast?"

"You can't believe all the things she told me about my dad, but the best thing is, she wants to take me to Ohio tomorrow to meet him. She said she called him and he's willing to see me." Adam was so excited. I wanted to say, *I spent all that time wanting you to come home and now you're out, and you're spending time with people you hardly know.* But I didn't.

"If that's what you want to do, Adam."

*Annette Bergman*

"Mom, I really do. I never thought I might get to meet him. Did you know he's a millionaire?"

"No, Adam, I didn't know that."

# Chapter 33

I sat in what seemed like a demolished living room waiting for Adam to come home. I was wondering how the meeting had gone between Adam and his biological father. Would he hate me for not letting him know about his father earlier in his life? I was still certain that I had made the right decision. Clay had been as good a father as he knew how to be, and that was the problem. All he knew was what he had been taught by his own upbringing, which had had a lot of harmful half-truths in it. *Be bigger than your problems;* that must have contributed to his eating disorder—he was much too heavy—and it seemed like he just kept getting bigger by the year. He had probably been just little more than a baby when he first heard that bit of so-called wisdom, and in a child's mind he probably figured the only way to be bigger than your problems was to get large physically.

*A man doesn't cry* was just as damaging. No wonder he hadn't cried at his father's funeral; his mother would have thought him some kind of a weakling. Imagine going though life not being able to express your emotions. I heard his mother say more than once *Clayton is a good boy.* That probably caused some sneaking around, and God knows what else when you have to live up to *Clayton is a good boy* all your life. No one is perfect, and how hard it must have been for Clay.

Oh, to be able to turn back the pages of time and undo all the damage. Maybe if Clay had stayed with us he could have benefited from some personal counseling. Being in counseling had helped me to realize that parents make many mistakes. They have no written rules to live by, or raise their children by. How I wished there had been more counseling sooner in our marriage. Maybe then we would have still been together as a family instead of starting out to make a new life.

Looking around at all the packed boxes I wondered if it were like taking the old baggage into a new life or if Adam and I had enough new knowledge and faith to stick to a change, for a better life.

How I hoped that this move back to Georgia was the right thing to do for both of us.

The lawsuits were settled, Adam was out of jail, the house was sold and most of the unwanted things had been sold in a garage sale. The movers were coming tomorrow and the following day we would be on our way.

Brian had been extremely good to me through the accident, and I wondered if I would ever work for anyone who was as helpful as he had been. He had loaned me money, showed properties to my clients, written up the sale and wouldn't even take half of it. Most brokers wouldn't have been that considerate. I definitely was going to miss working with Brian.

There had been great support from our friends when the accident had happened. Just thinking about it brought tears to my eyes. Even though I had no blood relatives in Kokomo I felt like I had friends who were as good to me as some of my family. I felt sad that I was leaving what had been home for me for more than 20 years. "I can't think about that now."

It was going to be harder to leave, than I had anticipated. It was too late to dig in the garden, all of my sewing was packed away and I wasn't sure what do with the feeling I was having, couldn't think about that now. I burst out in tears and sobbed like a brokenhearted child. I cried for my dead mother, I cried for my failed marriage and I cried because I would never feel Clay's strong arms around me again.

I cried for the grandchild who had died and I would never know. I cried for the hurt I had caused my son by not letting him know about his father. I cried because I was leaving the house that I had called home for so long, and I wondered if I would ever have another house I loved as much as I loved this one. I went to bed with a handful of tissues and cried some more, falling into such a deep sleep that I didn't hear Adam come home.

I awoke surprised that I had gone to sleep, my eyes swollen, Charlie Cropper was playing his usual beautiful country music on WWKI. I had awoken to Charlie's voice and music for as long as Clay and I had been married. It was one of the many little things he had contributed to our marriage. Waking to music in the morning had been a great way to start the day, and we had started all of our married days with music. Charlie had a knack for playing the best of country music in the mornings.

I quickly ran upstairs to see if Adam had come home. He was asleep and I thanked God for bringing him back home to me safely. I went back downstairs into the kitchen to put on the coffee, thinking that this was next to the last day that I would be getting up to Charlie's country music and putting on the coffee in my dream home.

Adam slept late and I was anxious to hear all about his meeting with his father, I was thinking of getting him up when I heard the water running in the upstairs bathroom. Thank goodness he was finally awake. Shortly I heard him coming down the stairs.

"Good morning. I didn't hear you come in last night, it must have been late."

"It was somewhere around two-thirty. I didn't realize that it took so long to drive to Cleveland," he said as he poured himself a cup of coffee.

"Well, how did it go?"

"There's so much to tell you, Mom." He sipped the coffee.

"When we first got there, Faye left me at a restaurant while she went over to see my dad. She was supposed to come back for me after she talked to him. Instead, I was sitting there waiting, when a tall blonde haired girl came over to me and said, 'Yep, you're my brother!'

"She looked a lot like me. She was tall and thin and had reddish-blonde hair. She said Dad had sent her over to get me. When we got to the house, Jack and Faye were still standing out in the driveway talking. Jack came over immediately and said, 'You can tell you're a Campbell,' then he shook my hand and then gave me a hug. I really hadn't expected such a warm welcome. In fact, I'm not sure what I had expected. We stood out in the driveway talking for a few minutes, and he invited us to come into his home. He has a real nice house. He asked Judy his sister to show us around and he started making phone calls, telling whoever was on the other end to come over he had a surprise for them. It turned out to be a surprise for me, too. I have two sisters and two brothers. When he hung up the phone he wanted to show me his game room. Your picture was on the wall and it had half of a dollar bill in one corner of the picture. There were several pictures of women there and two others had half of a dollar bill next to them. Jack said 'These are all my women.'

"Faye's picture was there, but there wasn't a dollar bill next to hers. I didn't want to ask what that meant, so I didn't say anything."

"You're kidding. He still has a picture of me on his wall?"

"He does, I was kinda overwhelmed by everything. His sister lives with him.  He has this huge house and has a maid."

"It seems he is very successful. He owns his own insurance company and has several agents working for him. I talked to the kids mostly. We were trying to figure out the order that all of us were born and Jack sat down at the computer to put it all together."

"I guess Jack Lee is the oldest, then me, then A.J. was next, but no one wanted to talk about him, then Judy and then Jamie. After her is Justin and then Jacob. There was a young girl there with a baby and I wondered if that was the latest one, but I didn't want to ask so I didn't say anything," Adam said.

"Faye was ready to come back She wasn't enjoying herself at all. Jack wanted us to spend the night, but Faye wouldn't hear of it. We didn't stay that long, Faye wanted to leave. Everyone was having a good time. But Faye, she seemed upset. I felt sorry for her. I think she was feeling the loss of her son. Her oldest son wasn't there. He lives in another town. Did you know that Jack's aunt raised her oldest son?"

"I knew she would take care of him sometimes when he was just a baby. The only time I heard from Jack was when one of the children was born, but that was after he married.

"For some reason every time he and his wife would have a baby he would give me a call. I tried to act like I wasn't interested, and after several calls he quit calling until one day he called to say he was going to see me one way or another. You were about twelve years old then."

"Mom, he didn't have a bad word to say about you."

"Adam, I'm glad you got a chance to meet your biological father and I hope you don't hate me for walking away and not having anything to do with him. I did what I thought was best at the time, and I hope you don't hold it against me."

"I understand why you did what you did, and I'll never hold it against you. I'm glad you raised me the way you did. I think of Clay as my real father. I just wish he hadn't walked away from us. I miss him," he said with tears in his eyes.

"Well, Adam, we have a lot of things left to do before we leave in the morning. We had better get busy. The movers will be here at noon and we need to be ready."

I had wished Clay hadn't have walked away, too, but I wasn't going to talk about that now. I was afraid I would start crying again and frankly I was tired of crying.

I went to the telephone to call Faye. "Hello, Faye, it's Paige. I just wanted to thank you for taking Adam to Ohio to meet his father. Who would have ever thought twenty years ago that you would be the one to bring the two of them face to face. I'm really grateful to you for doing that."

"I was glad to do it. After losing A.J., I didn't want you to lose Adam. After what he has been through I thought it might help for him to know the truth. He's a nice young man and I enjoyed spending time with him. We had a good trip and I hope this isn't the last time you and I talk. I would like to stay in touch with Adam. He looks so much like A.J."

I could hear the sadness in Faye's voice. "Faye, we'll stay in touch, and again thank you for being so good to Adam. We'll drop you a line when we get to Georgia"

The movers came and packed our things and early the next morning the two of us left behind bittersweet memories to pursue a new life.

# Chapter 34

FORSYTH PARK FOUNTAIN
SAVANNAH, GA.

The trip to Tybee was a relaxing drive and Adam and I talked of the future and what a new start in life would be like. The farther south I drove the warmer it became. It was dusk when we crossed the bridge into Savannah. "We're taking the long way around town. Mama always said, 'When the Dogwoods are blooming it's time for Paige to come home.' They aren't in full bloom now, and my mother is dead. I don't know if I'll ever get over her death. One thing is for sure, every time the dogwoods bloom, I'll think of Mama."

Adam reached over and squeezed my hand. "It's not going to be the same to come back to Tybee and not have Grandma here."

"Let's try to be strong for Grandpa and add a little happiness to his life."

The drive down Whitaker Street past Forsyth Park where the azaleas and wisteria are so beautiful in the spring made me feel like I had just been baptized. The southern air was warm and Savannah was beautiful. The azaleas and Palmetto trees along Victory Drive were in their splendor. It felt like a new life just being in such a beautiful city. As we drove on toward Tybee Island and crossed the Bull River bridge, the southern air was replaced with fresh salt air. It was a smell that was familiar to me and the scent brought with it a peace and contentment I knew only on Tybee Island. It had a feeling of contentment that lingers and makes a person feel welcome. It was good to be home again.

I was looking forward to seeing my Daddy, and Adam was happy just being free.

"Look, there's a ship in the channel." I had seen hundreds of ships, but each time had its own excitement. I wondered where the ship had come from and where it would be going once it returned to the ocean from the Savannah River. "That's a freighter," I said. "You can tell by the containers it has on it."

283

The air smelled of marsh and was moist, the sun had set and twilight cast a beautiful glow on the marsh. The palmettos were lining the roadway like sentinels standing guard over a special place. It was, indeed, special to me. I had come home again; this time to stay. I felt at peace. I was within miles of my father's house and the late evening darkness that was closing in was also closing a chapter of our lives that I didn't want to look back on.

Daddy was sitting in his chair when we entered the house. It was difficult for him to get up and down so he sat where he could watch the street and with a turn of his head he could see who was coming in the back door. His face looked happy, and there was a twinkle in his eye. He, too, was grateful to have his daughter home.


Adam found a job working in a restaurant and had energy to help around the house, too. My father was happy just having someone there with him. Dorothy had eventually gone back to Kentucky. Daddy had become lonely since Mama had died, and now he had someone to pick on. That had always been his way of showing affection. I hadn't realized how wrong that kind of affection was until Bob Lawson had pointed it out to me during counseling. Now it didn't seem to bother me since I understood my father better.

We had been back to Tybee several weeks when the dewberries began to ripen. On a few mornings Adam and I went berry picking. Neither one of us said anything about the last time we had picked berries together. We picked enough berries for pie and jam. I made a dewberry pie as soon as we returned home.

"I think you're burning something." Daddy called out.

I hurried to the kitchen. My cobbler had boiled over in the oven and smoke was everywhere.

"It's just like having your mother back in the kitchen. You both burn everything you cook."

"Well, Daddy, I have a solution to that," I replied.

"What's that?" he asked.

"I don't have to cook!" I smiled as I said it.

"It always tastes good," he said quickly, not wanting me to stop cooking. I leaned over and gave my father a big hug.

As soon as I had finished the dinner dishes I said. "Adam, don't you think we should unpack the rest of these boxes? They've been sitting here long enough."

Adam began taking things out of the boxes and handing them to me to put away. He unpacked a photo album and started to look through it. One page had a postcard from a motel in Greenfield, Indiana, a ticket stub to the 500 Race in Indianapolis dated May, 1964, a set of private's stripes from an Army uniform, and half of a dollar bill.

"Mom, what is this?" Adam asked, knowing it had something to do with his real father.

"What's what?" I answered while putting things on the shelf in the closet.

"This album."

I was happy to have Adam's help in unpacking and had forgotten about the album. My heart sank. Now I would have to explain everything to Adam. Walking over I took a place beside him and put my arm around him.

"Adam, I know this might be difficult for you to understand, but I just couldn't part with this album. It reminds me of the love I had for your father, and how wonderful young love can be. It also reminds me of the foolish mistakes I've made."

"Tell me about it," Adam said.

"I went to work for an insurance company years ago, and that's where I met your father. We started seeing one another and one weekend we went to the race. It was after he had finished boot camp and was on leave before he went to Texas. Your father gave me these private's stripes and this is the motel that we stayed in." I handed Adam the postcard dated May 15, 1964.

"I had waited for your father to finish boot camp before I told him I was pregnant. I didn't want to tell him while he was still in basic training, so when he came home on leave I told him the weekend we went to the Indianapolis 500. At first he denied that you were his child. I knew you were his because I hadn't been with anyone else. I knew how badly he treated Faye and I didn't want to be treated like that. He later left for Texas and these are the letters that he wrote to me while he was there. I have one here that made me think he was going to marry me when he came home."

Turning to the letter I was referring to, I handed it to my son. "The rest are letters he wrote to me while he was away, and the half of a dollar is what he gave me the last time I saw him. He had finished his training in Texas and had come home on leave. That's when I found out that Faye was pregnant for the second time. I told your father that I didn't ever want to see him again. He tore a dollar bill in half and said, 'Until we meet again.' I never saw him again until you were twelve years old. He used to call me from time to time, like every time he and his wife had another child."

Suddenly, my mind went back to a day when he called me when I was going for an interview for my first real estate job. I would never forget it. I was getting dressed and the phone rang.

"Hello."

"Hi, Sport."

"I can't believe it, how did you find me"

"I've always known where you where and what you were doing. I had my Aunt Catherine keep up with you for me. It's been twelve years since I last saw you and I'm going to see you today one way or another. Now, would you like to meet me somewhere or would you rather that I come to your home?" he said.

"Please, don't come here. Clay wouldn't like it. I have an interview at 10:00 this morning and I should be finished by 11:00. I'll meet you at the Golden Bear Restaurant. Just wait for me if I'm a little late. I'll be there."

"Oh, I'll wait. I've been waiting for twelve years. It's really good to hear your voice. I'll see you at 11:00."

I explained all of this to Adam then continued my narrative.

"I was excited. It was like Christmas. I could hardly wait until 11:00. I was glad I had made arrangements to see him in a public place. I was afraid if I saw him in private, I didn't know how I would react. I couldn't trust myself around your father, Adam. I loved him so much, and I could feel myself melt in his presence. We met at 11:00, and again I was thankful that I *was* in a public place. My heart was pounding, my hands were sweating, and I had to act like I was meeting someone who didn't mean anything to me. What I wanted to do was hug him and tell him how much I had missed him. But, I kept thinking, *I'm married now and this is unfair to Clay. He has tried to be a good father to Adam and I can't be unfaithful to him.* Jack and I talked about old times and old friends. He told me he had seen me one time at a department store when you were really small. He said Clay was with us so he didn't come over to talk."

I was starting to feel uncomfortable with these memories.

"Adam you need to know that your father was the love of my life, and I always felt like when I became pregnant with you that God gave me the best part of him. I've tried to love you enough for two people. But I'm sorry now that I never allowed you to get to know your father. But more than that, I'm sorry that the circumstances you were born under have caused you so much grief. Let's put this up. We can't change the past. What do you say we take a break and go for a walk on the beach?"

Adam agreed. But he really wanted to hear more about his real father.

"Daddy, Adam and I are going for a walk on the beach. We shouldn't be gone very long."

The two of us headed for the beach. We had walked for awhile before Adam said. "Mom, remember when you would come to visit me and we would talk about how I could repay you for all you've done for me?"

"Yes, I remember. You talked and I listened. You don't have to repay me. It's what a mother does. I don't expect any repayment."

"You stood by me even thought you didn't want me to have that car. I just want you to know how much I appreciate all you've done for me and I'm not upset that you didn't tell me about my father before you did. You did the best you knew at the time and that's all any of us can do. Mom, I'm sorry that this accident cost you your marriage."

"I've wondered about that a thousand times and finally one day I asked Bob Lawson. His theory was that Clay is a rescuer. He found a woman who was in need, and he helped me out. However, with a rescuer, once their victims are on their feet, the rescuer becomes threatened and no longer feels needed. The truth of the matter was that he didn't show me any attention. He spent all his time in the garage or wanted to go square dancing or deer hunting. By the time our relationship ended I had convinced myself that no one would ever want me again. After all, I had bought this man a new truck and had done everything I could to keep his love. The counselor said the things that I had done for Clay had destroyed his self-esteem and deep down he felt like Clay wanted to do those things for me. All I can say is, it's a shame that people aren't made to be evaluated and have counseling before they are allowed to get a divorce. I feel that if you can't work it out the first time you are married, you continue in relationships, and repeat the same mistakes. I don't think you want to hear all of my theories. In fact I have so many theories now, I'm positive you don't want to know about them all."

"Sounds like you tried to figure it out."

"I just know that it all made me a little wiser and I look at men completely different now, and I don't have to have a man to be a whole person."

"It's getting dark, Mom, We need to go back home."

The two of us walk in the dusty night's light back to my childhood home where my world, with my son and my father were all I needed.

# Chapter 35

In 1993 I called Jim Fleming's office.

"Hi, this is Paige Mitchell. I was wondering if you still had the records of my son's accidents in your files. His name is Adam Mitchell."

"I remember that name. Let me check. Yes, we still have his file. What is it that you need?" a friendly voice said.

"I was wondering if you could send me anything that pertains to my son's accident. Any depositions or perhaps the reconstruction reports. All that you can find," I answered.

"We'd be happy to. Where would you like for me to this mailed this to."

I gave my P.O. Box number on Tybee Island, Georgia.

"If you need anything else, just let us know," said the friendly voice.

When the package arrived with the information I just put it aside. Wondering why I couldn't forget about the accident, I didn't have the nerve to start reading what might be in the envelope. I put it with the trial transcript that I had acquired through a girl who worked in the courthouse in Peru and would have done anything I wanted her to do for a price.

It was a rainy Sunday afternoon in 1996 and I was feeling rather depressed. It was a good time to read depressing things. I closed the door to my sewing room and sat down. I started with the trial transcript. I knew very little about law and even less about criminal law. I would read and wonder about some of the procedures. Like why was my son's name in the paper when a juvenile was supposed to be protected? How could a policeman testify on someone else's behalf. Wasn't that hearsay?

It was getting dark outside, but I had just about finished the trial transcript. I forced myself to finish it and to open the envelope that had been sent to me from Jim Fleming office. I looked through the papers. There was a report from the police with a list of names of witnesses.

"Wait a minute. The police testified that there had been only one witness: a truck driver. Even the State Police had testified on his behalf at the trial." One name in particular stood out at me. I wrote down his name, address and phone number. My mind was made up. I was going to call. I knew it had been fourteen years and my chances of finding this man were slim, but my mind kept saying *call him, call him.*

I wanted to wait until I was at work to make the call. I dialed the number and got a recording. "Hi, this is Paige Mitchell. I'm trying to reach a Jose' Rodrigues. Would you please return my call." I left the phone number.

Several hours later the phone rang.

"Hello, Heritage Real Estate. May I help you."

"I'm calling for Paige Mitchell."

"This is Paige Mitchell."

"Hi. This is Jose' Rodrigues."

"Yes, Mr. Rodrigues, I wasn't sure I would find you after all this time. I hope you can help me. I just read a report about an accident on U.S. 31."

He interrupted. "Where the state Trooper was killed?"

"Yes."

"Oh, Lady. You don't know the feelings you are stirring up to me," he said.

"I didn't call you to upset you. I was wondering if you were a witness to that accident."

"Yes, I was. In fact, Officer Robert Sabatini from the State Police post came to my house and I told him before he turned the recorder on that I would be telling him some things he might not want on tape and he told me to tell it as it happened."

"And how was that Mr. Rodrigues?" I asked.

"I was behind this 18 wheeler and I saw a car coming up behind me and another one in front of me pull out really slow from the median. I was wondering what he was doing because he was barely moving. I could tell the car behind me was coming up fast, and I was wondering what I might need to be doing. It all happened very quickly."

"Did the trooper have his red lights on?" I asked.

"No. He did not."

"Are you sure?"

"Absolutely. I didn't know it was a trooper until I got to the wreck.

I pulled the young man from the car. He looked wild. I didn't know if he was hurt or not and I didn't want him to move, so I was holding him down, and all of a sudden there were police all over him. They started beating him. I begged them not to, and they told me to leave. They treated me like a no good Chicano. I felt really bad for the boy. I tried to help him and they wouldn't let me. Do you remember the Rodney King case?" He asked.

"Yes, I do."

"Well, it was just like that. I don't remember if they were beating him with flashlights or Billy clubs. There was one really big guy. I think he was a Kokomo policeman. He was the main one. I believe if that boy had gotten up, they would have shot him. I think about the boy a lot." You could hear his voice breaking. "And I think about his mother," he added.

"You're talking to his mother," I answered. The sobs came unbidden from Mr. Rodrigues. When he had gotten some composure, he said, "I wanted so badly to help him, and they wouldn't let me. I feel guilty. I let him down."

"Please, Mr. Rodrigues, don't feel guilty. You did all you could do," I said. "I've always known that something wasn't right with Adam's case. Here the Indiana State police had a witness and even had your testimony and claimed that they only had one witness and that the Trooper had his lights on."

"They were not on and I am positive about it. I can't believe they didn't tell anyone about my statement. That is just like the police. This is America, but we really aren't *free*. They do as they please and we have to take it. Tell me, how is your son doing now?"

"Well, Mr. Rodrigues, he's still having problems living with what he did. Last Thanksgiving he shot himself. He survived and he's going to be okay. I think he will get over this accident, now that the truth has surfaced. I can't thank you enough for taking the time to talk with me about this."

"If I'm ever in Kokomo, could I meet with you?"

"You certainly can. I would be proud to meet you face to face and hopefully one day you can meet my son, too," I said.

"I would like that very much," Mr. Rodrigues said.

I thanked him again and hung up the phone. I, too, felt a sense of relief. It was as though I could finally put the accident to rest. I knew in my heart that my son had not been fleeing the police. I knew that if he had seen a red light he would have stopped. The police who were behind him were several miles behind him when the accident happened and he didn't know they were there.

That evening I called Adam. I told him how I had sat down and read all of the trial transcript and then looked at the information that the girl in Jim Fleming's office had sent me. Then I told him about calling Mr. Rodrigues and what he had to say.

"I can't believe that I have been beating myself up all these years for what happened and it was just as much his fault as it was mine. Mom, you don't know how much this means to me...I would like to meet Mr. Rodrigues someday to thank him personally for what he tried to do for me."

He paused a moment in thought before continuing.

"Mom, why would the police do things like that?"

"I'm sure for every bad one there are one hundred good ones. I suppose they think they are the judge, jury and executioner. Adam, we can't waste our time wondering why. We have to learn from our mistakes, and ask God to forgive us. Each one of us has to answer to God one day. I was hoping that knowing the truth about this accident would help you forgive yourself and to also know that God has us go through some things in life for a purpose. If you believe in the predestination, then there are no accidents. Just God giving us different direction to lead us to the place in life that we are supposed to be.

"Adam, just trust in God and look at each day as a new beginning and life will just get better and better." I paused to let him consider that.

Adam, Jesus once said, 'You are the ones who justify yourselves in the eyes of men, but God knows your hearts. What is highly valved among men is detestable in God's sight.' Adam we must forgive in order to be forgiven. Please forgive the people who withheld the truth and forgive Clay for walking away. I also need you to forgive me for the circumstances of your birth. I know God gave you to me for a purpose and I love you very much."

"Have you ever heard the hymn *It is well with my soul*?"

It was written by a man who had just lost his entire family and he was on a ship going back to Europe when he wrote these words:

When peace like a river, attendeth my way,
when sorrows like sea billows roll;
whatever my lot, thou hast taught me to say,
it is well, it is well with my soul.
It is well with my soul, it is well, it is well with my soul.
"Adam we must make this well with our souls."

The State Police post that investigated Adam's accident is the same State Police post in Peru, Indiana that investigated the murder of prosecutor James Grund, Adam's prosecutor. A book entitled *Deadly Seduction* gives the account of Mr. Grund's murder. The State police withheld the results of a polygraph test given to Mr. Grund's son.

Grund's wife was convicted of the murder and is serving a life sentence.

*Annette Bergman*

# About the Author

"My friend and writing student Annette has gone through a life-altering experience and come out of it a more positive person that anyone could expect. She fought the court systems, survived bad marriages, overcame the stigma of an imprisoned son, and endured times of financial strain. Through it all she was focused, goal-oriented, and optimistic. She's one in a million."

—Dennis E. Hensley, Ph.D.

I would like to thank all of the people who encouraged me during the long process of writing Return to Tybee. A special thanks to my husband for his support and belief in me, and for all of the hours I withdrew myself from our lives to get this book finished.

Mostly I want to thank my family members for all of the love and support they gave me during the aftermath of my son's accident. I am eternally grateful.

I wish to thank Carl Thompson for his generosity for the use of his renditions in this book.

A special thanks to Diane Holmes for her friendship and encouragement during the writing of this book, Also for helping me to experience my first Writers Retreat in her home in Texas.

To Dr. Dennis Hensley for his editing skills, his friendship and most of all for all of the side bar comments that gave me the encouragement to finish this book.

May God bless each one who has helped me along the way.

Printed in the United States
1166500004B/52-1008